Advance praise for *Overcoming School Anxiety*

"*Overcoming School Anxiety* is empowering for both parent and child. I wish I had had these practical solutions when my son was younger. Anxiety and its causes are defined clearly and made simple to understand. Among the exercises given, the breathing exercise is my favorite. It applies in both scholastic and social situations. I can see these techniques even help my son with his anxiety on the pitching mound. I look forward to sharing this insightful and helpful book with friends who struggle with anxiety."
—Betty Ann Castaneda, parent, California

"I am a stay-at-home mom of two wonderful daughters, ages 3 and 5. My 5-year-old has already exhibited signs of school anxiety. She is extremely shy and introverted and has a difficult time forming new relationships with her classmates. I am very excited to be reading *Overcoming School Anxiety* at this time. I feel it will be an important tool that I will use constantly to deal with her issues. I especially like the way the table of contents is written. Easy to skim to find the exact topic I need. The most important concept in the book that will help my daughter is the stress level at home. We constantly procrastinate in the mornings and always seem to be scrambling to get out the door. I didn't realize the effect this had on my daughter's anxiety (I thought it only made me feel stressed and anxious!). I see this book as an invaluable tool that will stay by my bedside throughout my daughter's school career."
—Lisa Nero, parent, California

"When your child has school anxiety, sometimes, try as you might, you just can't understand your child's behavior. And that is very frustrating. Diane Peters Mayer's clear explanations, perfect examples, and practical steps can change all of that frustration."
—Farrell Silverberg, Ph.D., N.C.Psy.A., psychologist, psychoanalyst, and author, *Make the Leap: A Practical Guide to Breaking the Patterns That Hold You Back*

"This book is an informative, concise, and practical guide to anxiety and many other important issues of today's youth. It provided me with effective, easy to follow and implement solutions that helped my students. I would strongly recommend it to any teacher or parent as a practical guidebook to better understanding and aiding our youth."
—Waldemar Plichta, ME, foreign language teacher, Cedar Crest High School, Lebanon, Pennsylvania

OVERCOMING
SCHOOL
ANXIETY

OVERCOMING
SCHOOL
ANXIETY

How to Help Your Child Deal with
Separation, Tests, Homework, Bullies,
Math Phobia, and Other Worries

DIANE PETERS MAYER

ᴬMACOM

American Management Association
NEW YORK • ATLANTA • BRUSSELS • CHICAGO • MEXICO CITY • SAN FRANCISCO
SHANGHAI • TOKYO • TORONTO • WASHINGTON, D.C.

This publication is designed to provide accurate and authoritative
information in regard to the subject matter covered. It is sold with
the understanding that the publisher is not engaged in rendering
legal, accounting, or other professional service. If legal advice or
other expert assistance is required, the services of a competent
professional person should be sought.

Library of Congress Cataloging-in-Publication Data

Peters Mayer, Diane.
    Overcoming school anxiety : how to help your child deal with separation, tests, homework,
bullies, math phobia, and other worries / Diane Peters Mayer.
        p.   cm.
    Includes bibliographical references and index.
    ISBN 978-0-8144-7446-4 (pbk.)
    1. Anxiety in children.   I. Title.

BF723.A5P47   2008
649'.154—dc22   2008009563

Printing number

10   9   8   7   6   5   4   3   2

This book is dedicated to Benzion Rappoport, Ph.D.—
humanist, master therapist, scholar, teacher, and musician.
You were, and always will be, a driving force in my journey as
a therapist and writer.

Contents

CHAPTER 1 • What Is School Anxiety? 1

anxiety is a normal aspect of being human • positive and negative effects on mental and physical functioning • definition of school anxiety and discussion of symptoms • causes and effects of school anxiety • short- and long-term effects of school anxiety

CHAPTER 2 • Anxiety Is a Mind-Body Experience 10

examination of stress and children's reaction to stress • physiological effects of anxiety • discussion of the nervous system • fight-or-flight and relaxation responses • matching physical, mental, and emotional anxiety symptoms to physiological changes • reasons for chronic anxiety • development of an anxiety disorder • guidelines for professional help • list of common anxiety disorders • ways to help children deal with stress

CHAPTER 3 • Help! My Child Won't Go to School 20

causes and effects of school refusal • discussion of why leaving home can be difficult • childhood fears of parents dying while child is at school • childhood worries about not "fitting in" • definition of separation anxiety disorder (SAD) and its symptoms • guidelines for preventing and easing the anxiety of school refusal • exercises, techniques, and parental guidelines

CHAPTER 4 • My Child Can't Stop Worrying 31

sources of childhood worry (testing, homework assignments, teachers, socializing) • explanation of chronic worry and generalized anxiety disorder (GAD) • effects of worry on school performance • tips to help children stop worrying • exercises, techniques, and parental guidelines

CHAPTER 5 • My Child Panics and Avoids Situations 42

definition of panic disorders and symptoms • causes and effects of panic • discussion of agoraphobia and its effect on attending school • tips on helping children cope with panic • exercises and examples

CHAPTER 6 • My Child Fears People, Places, and Things 55

definitions of social phobia and simple phobia and explanation of childhood symptoms • causes of phobias • examination of phobia's effects on school experience • information on types of professional treatment • exercises and techniques to help stop phobias • tips for creating a systematic desensitization program • guidelines for helping children cope with phobias

CHAPTER 7 • My Child Has Homework Anxiety 67

guidelines if child dreads homework • how to ease homework anxiety • creating a comfortable homework space • breaking down the homework load • answers to common questions for parents of a school-anxious child • exercises and techniques for conquering homework anxiety • tips for making learning exciting for children

CHAPTER 8 • My Child Has Test Anxiety 77

definition of test anxiety and discussion of its symptoms • how test anxiety builds up • explanation of physical, mental, and emotional effects of pretest anxiety • symptoms of test anxiety • exercises, test-taking techniques, and parental guidelines

CHAPTER 9 • My Child Is a Perfectionist 88

definition of perfectionism • characteristics and causes of perfectionism • link between perfectionism and anxiety • guidelines to help children become less rigid in their thinking and ease the anxiety associated with perfectionism • exercises and techniques include learning how to relax, "letting go," and practicing making mistakes

CHAPTER 10 • Building Your Child's Self-Esteem 100

definition of self-esteem and self-worth • causes of low self-esteem • negative self-talk • guidelines to build up a child's self-esteem • easy projects and exercises for parents and children to work on together • tips on how to use a child's strengths to build self-esteem

CHAPTER 11 • My Child Is Being Bullied 112

definition of bullying • differences between girl and boy bullies • link between bullying and school anxiety • how to help children cope with bullies • when to step in to help your child and when to contact the school • what to do if your child is the bully • exercises to help children take control of the bullying situation • how to help your school enact an antibullying program

CHAPTER 12 • Parental and Family Conflict and Issues 123

types of family conflict that create anxiety and lead to school anxiety • unique ways children handle family conflict • symptoms of family conflict such as anxiety, behavior problems, and poor grades • guidelines to help a child deal with divorce, death of a parent, and moving to a new home and school

CHAPTER 13 • My Child Has Learning, Physical, or Emotional Challenges 135

physical and learning challenges that make the school experience difficult • link between learning challenges, physical challenges, and anxiety • information on how to prepare children for the school environment academically and emotionally • tips and exercises to teach children how to cope and thrive at school

CHAPTER 14 • Learn to Breathe to Feel at Ease 147

breathing and anxiety • explanation of belly breathing (diaphragmatic breathing) and its positive effect on the relaxation response • physical, mental, and emotional effects of belly breathing • how belly breathing can stop school anxiety • guide-lines and instructions for practicing belly breathing • how to use belly breathing in stressful school situations

CHAPTER 15 • "Be Present" for School Success 159

how to live in the moment • how being in the moment can reduce school anxiety for test taking, homework, or speaking up in class • guidelines for practicing living in the moment • instructions for teaching children to live in the moment • exer-cises for a variety of school situations

CHAPTER 16 • Learning to Let Go and Flow 169

teaching your child to face fears to reduce anxiety • description of the white-knuckle response and how it increases your child's school anxiety • instructions on helping your child ride out anxiety when it surfaces in school • how to help your child to "loosen and float" at school • guidelines for loosening anxiety's grip on your child's mind • exercises for facing fears and letting them go

CHAPTER 17 • Eat Right to Feel Right 180

link between nutrition and increased or decreased anxiety • effects on school performance of a child's diet that is high in processed and fatty foods • how vitamin and mineral deficiencies cause anxiety • guidelines for choosing a diet to help prevent and ease anxiety • types of professional help available for parents • suggestions for helping your school change its lunch menus and snacks • studies showing how diet can help decrease anxiety and behavioral problems

CHAPTER 18 • Getting Physical with Your Child 191

how exercise reduces anxiety • why exercise has a positive effect on anxiety and anxiety disorders • description of kinds of exercises paired with developmental stages • guidelines for beginning an exercise program for your child, yourself, and even your whole family

CHAPTER 19 • What Are Traditional Medical Treatments for Children? 201

discussion of traditional medical treatments such as medication and numerous psychotherapies • use of antidepressants in children • what happens in a psycho-therapist's or psychiatrist's office • types of mental health practitioners who practice therapy • kinds of therapy available for children • discussion of the downside of psychotropic medications for children

CHAPTER 20 • What Are Alternative Treatments for Children? 211

description of complementary and alternative medicine (CAM) • discussion of yoga, herbs, and acupuncture • practitioners of CAM such as holistic medical physicians and alternative practitioners

Foreword

THE GREATEST GIFT TO ANY PARENT IS HOPE FOR IMPROVEMENT when his or her child is struggling. For parents of the 6 million children who suffer from school anxiety, an increased understanding and the formulation of a clear, concise treatment plan can greatly diminish frustration levels for both the child and the parent.

In this valuable and highly readable book, Diane Peters Mayer provides a sensitive, useful guide that equips parents with strategies to help their child. She normalizes the often overwhelming challenge of dealing with incapacitating school anxiety and formulates practical, solution-focused directives to help lessen worries, phobias, and performance issues. Rather than the problem ruling the child, she provides the tools for the child to rule the problem.

Through better understanding of the physiological, psychological, and behavioral components of anxiety, parents can create a framework to help their child identify the symptoms of progressive worry and its debilitating consequences. Common difficulties including homework and test anxiety, separation issues, and refusal to attend school are addressed with simple, effective exercises that parents can utilize at home with their child. Bullying, social and familial stressors, anxiety disorders, and phobias are discussed and additional important attention is given to learning, physical, and emotional challenges. Parents will be able to assess whether their child's worry is appropriate and productive or chronic and dysfunctional.

To help parents navigate the often turbulent waters of school anxiety, Diane has created a self-help program that can be instituted directly with their child. With pertinent, empathetic directives, this book can assist parents in knowing what to say, how to elicit professional help, and perhaps, most important, how to teach their children to manage anxiety themselves. By learning to master school anxiety, both the child and the parents regain a sense of control over their lives. Lending her professional experience in working with families affected by school anxiety, Diane encourages parents to utilize proven techniques for reducing anxiety. Relaxation and mindfulness exercises, role-playing, and the use of systematic desensitization are presented with detailed explanations. Multiple approaches are presented for a variety of situations. Each chapter provides step-by-step instructions that are easy to understand and practice in both school and home settings. The importance of nutrition and exercise are given special attention along with the many treatment options available within traditional and alternative medicine. Treatment modalities including psychotherapy, holistic techniques, and medication are outlined in full. Parents will learn which treatments are best suited to their child's needs.

With wisdom and concrete, practical examples, Diane has written a self-help guide that parents will value as a treasured resource. This book brings hope to parents and empowers them in helping their child move toward productive academic, social, and psychological ways of living.

—Deirdre Shaffer, MSW

Preface

DEAR PARENT,

The book you hold in your hands contains information and a self-help program that is a beginning point for you to help your child overcome school anxiety. As you can attest, school anxiety creates distress for your child and causes disruption in your family. *Overcoming School Anxiety* lays out the many reasons children become anxious in the learning environment and teaches you ways your child can become calm, manage the homework load, do well on tests, make friends, and feel good about himself or herself in school.

I have been developing the Overcoming School Anxiety Program throughout my eighteen years as a psychotherapist in private practice in Doylestown, Pennsylvania, working with school-anxious children and their parents. However, the real beginnings of this program come out of my own painful experiences with school anxiety. Although not formally diagnosed with a learning disability, as an adult I finally put a name to the struggles I had with math that could make school a living hell. Called dyscalculia, the condition is dyslexia with numbers and mathematical patterns. I also suffered from separation anxiety disorder in the early grades in elementary school, and all the way up until high school, I was considered an underachiever. I'm smart, but school anxiety buried my potential. When I had children, my youngest daughter was diagnosed with dyslexia in first grade. I know firsthand how it feels to be a parent with a child who struggled in school.

As a psychotherapist, I made anxiety disorders my specialty, and I am passionate about helping children overcome school anxiety. It took discipline and hard work to accept, face, and eventually conquer my own school anxiety. Your child can, too, with your patience, support, and determination—*Overcoming School Anxiety* will help you do it.

Throughout the book, the vignettes of children with school anxiety mainly come from children and parents whom I have worked with over the years. A small number are the children of friends. Names and all identifying information have been changed to ensure confidentiality. Thanks to them all.

—Diane Peters Mayer, MSW

Acknowledgments

I CAN NEVER SAY ENOUGH ABOUT MY WONDERFUL AGENT, JACKY Sach—she works hard for her writers. AMACOM Books has been a dream publisher to work with. Thanks to Adrienne Hickey, executive editor (retired), who initially believed in my book, and to Christina M. Parisi, executive editor, because of her excitement about the book, and for her expert insight and suggestions. And many thanks to Erika Spelman, associate editor, and Mary Miller, copyeditor, and to the unnamed AMACOM editors and staff for their hard work in making *Overcoming School Anxiety* possible. Deepest appreciation to Kristin Kwack, MS, RD, LDN, licensed nutritionist, for her input and expertise in Chapter 17, "Eat Right to Feel Right," and to Deirdre Shaffer, MSW, for writing the foreword.

To my husband and children for their continued support and understanding when I'm locked away in front of my computer meeting a deadline.

And to all the parents and their school-anxious children who have allowed me the honor of working with them in my therapy practice. As much as I have helped them to overcome their anxiety, they have helped me, too, in my continued growth as a therapist.

How to Use the Overcoming School Anxiety Program

OVERCOMING SCHOOL ANXIETY IS FILLED WITH INFORMATION THAT explains why children develop school anxiety. It also includes a program to help your child take control of anxiety and overcome it. In order to get the maximum results from the program, use the following guidelines:

1. Read through the table of contents to get an overall idea of the content of each chapter.
2. Zero in on the problems your child is experiencing, but also read the exercises at the end of each chapter for possible adaptation to your child's specific problems.
3. Take your time learning the exercises before you teach them to your child.
4. For faster results, make practice part of your child's daily routine.
5. Keep an "Overcoming School Anxiety Journal" to keep materials handy and to chart progress. Use a three-hole loose-leaf binder to make it easy to add new information. Date all materials so your child can look back to see how far he or she has come.
6. Help your child open up to the program, explaining that overcoming school anxiety takes practice and time, and that some of the exercises may be difficult to learn, but he or she can do it.
7. Have your child examined by your family physician before beginning the exercise part of the program.

CHAPTER 1

What Is School Anxiety?

ᕙᕗ

E VERYONE EXPERIENCES ANXIETY. AND MANY ADULTS AND CHIL-
dren experience quite a bit of stress in their daily lives that can
lead to more anxiety. There are many causes of school anxiety,
and children who have it may feel stressed out and unhappy five days a
week, nine months out of the year.

*Chuck, a fifth grader, has severe test anxiety that has been building
for days about an upcoming social studies test. As soon as he gets
out of bed on the morning of the test, he begins to think about it,
which causes his stomach to knot, his breathing to become shallow,
and his heart to pound. By the time Chuck sits down to breakfast,
his head is aching and he says he feels sick and wants to stay home.*

*Mika, in third grade, is being bullied and ostracized by a popular
group of girls whom she would like to be part of. They are nice to
her one day, but either don't talk to her or make fun of her the
next. Not knowing how this group will treat her from day to day
has Mika anxious almost all of the time. Every morning is a fight
just to get her out of bed and to the school bus on time, leaving
Mika and her parents exhausted.*

Children who are stressed about school on a daily basis become
anxious. They have to contend with the physical and mental manifestations of anxiety, which are uncomfortable, even distressing at times. In

this chapter you will learn how and why anxiety begins, what the symptoms of anxiety are, the effects of school anxiety, and how to begin to help your child.

Is Anxiety Always a Bad Thing?

Anxiety is a normal aspect of life and of being human, and it has a positive side to it, too. In order to have a zest for life, to go after dreams, to be mentally alert, and to achieve goals, anxiety is one of the driving forces that can help. Although that adrenaline rush is necessary to reach one's personal best, anxiety needs to be channeled for positive use.

> *Conrad, in sixth grade, has been playing the cello since third grade. He is talented, loves to practice, and is one of the soloists in his school orchestra. Starting a day or two before each concert, his stomach tightens up whenever he thinks about playing. A few hours before the concert, he feels jumpy and is unable to relax. He rehearses his solo over and over again in his mind. Minutes before his solo, stress hormones course through his body, his breathing becomes rapid, and all his senses are heightened. But instead of causing him to fall apart with anxiety, these physical changes sharpen his abilities, and he plays his part perfectly and with intense feeling. The audience goes wild after he finishes.*

Every performer, every person who wants to reach optimal performance, must learn how to take control of anxiety instead of being controlled by it, and use it in a positive way to enhance his or her life. Anxiety is also a motivator for making necessary life changes. For example, if your sixth-grade child underachieves because she doesn't feel like putting out an effort, but begins to worry about not making the grade in middle school, then her anxiety can jump-start her into becoming a good student.

Anxiety is also a normal response to life situations, such as experiencing the death of a loved one, having an illness, experiencing parental divorce, starting at a new school, taking a test, or getting the lead in the school play, which all create normal levels of anxiety and response.

Anxiety Differs from Fear

The words *fear* and *anxiety* are often used interchangeably, but they have different meanings. Fear is something external, specific, and definable. For example, if your child is waiting at the school bus stop and a car veers in her direction, her brain will instantly signal to her body, "Danger!" In a split second, her brain sends messages to her legs to jump out of the way to safety. The fear of being hurt by the car can be explained in specific terms. If you ask her, she'll say she was afraid and reacted by jumping out of the way.

Anxiety, on the other hand, is nonspecific; it's intangible in nature. There is no real bodily danger. For example, if your child is afraid to leave home to go to school, and you question why, he may not be able to give you a concrete answer, because anxious feelings are often hard to define. Maybe he fears something will happen to you when he is gone, or you will forget to pick him up at the bus stop, even though that has never happened. The "what-ifs"—the intense worry about the possibility that those things might happen—are what cause anxiety, making it very difficult for him to separate from you even for a few hours.

What Happens When Anxiety Turns Negative?

Anxiety becomes a problem when it causes emotional pain and suffering and disrupts your child's ability to function well at school and in daily life. When anxiety becomes that severe and chronic it is called a *disorder*. If your child has severe school anxiety, she will be limited in every area of development in her life because of the intensity of the feelings and symptoms. Anxiety disorders affect over 20 million adults, adolescents, and children in the United States, making it the number one mental health issue. Americans spend billions of dollars annually trying to alleviate anxious suffering by traditional and alternative modes of treatment.

Over 6 million school-age children suffer from school anxiety, trying to cope with physical and mental symptoms that are upsetting, even terrifying, at times.

What Is Anxiety?

Anxiety is defined as a state of intense agitation, foreboding, tension, and dread, occurring from a real or perceived threat of impending danger. The experience of anxiety is unique for each person, but it does have general physical and emotional characteristics.

It is important to note that the physical and mental symptoms of anxiety such as rapid heartbeat, stomachaches, and headaches are also found in many other medical conditions, like heart problems. If you, your child, or anyone in your family experiences persistent physical complaints, don't assume the cause is stress related but have the person checked by your family physician immediately.

Anxiety is a mind-body reaction that occurs instantaneously, and its effects are felt physiologically, behaviorally, and psychologically all at the same time. There are dozens of symptoms of anxiety that range from mild, such as having butterflies before answering a question in class, to severe, such as blanking out or having a panic attack when called to the board to solve a problem. It is important for you to be familiar with the symptoms of anxiety so you can explain to your child what is happening to him when he gets anxious. For example, if your child understands that the intense adrenaline rush he feels when anxiety hits cannot harm him, it may prevent his anxiety from spiraling out of control into a panic attack—instead he could learn to say to himself, "I know this is just a chemical in my body that is making me feel bad, but it can't really hurt me." Physical symptoms include the following:

- Shallow breathing and hyperventilation
- Intense rush of adrenaline and other stress hormones
- Pounding heartbeat, heart palpitations, and sweating

- Shaky limbs and trembling
- Body and muscle tension
- Dry mouth
- Headaches
- Nausea, diarrhea, and/or vomiting

Other physical manifestations of anxiety include skin eruptions, hives and rashes, fatigue, and eating and sleeping problems. The mental and emotional symptoms are equally distressing and include feeling overwhelmed, loss of concentration, feeling out of control, helplessness, hopelessness, anger, and shame. Behaviors in your child to watch for include acting-out behaviors such as angry outbursts and tantrums; refusal to go to school or to do homework; crying; inability to sleep; curtailment of activities; and avoidance of social situations, places, and certain people.

What Is School Anxiety?

School anxiety is being used as a broad term in this book. It refers, in part, to the problems from home that children bring to school including having an anxiety disorder; being learning disabled; or dealing with family issues, such as divorce or childhood trauma. However, the school environment can be a problematic place, too, with its emphasis on evaluation, achievement, and testing. Other factors might include peer pressure, being bullied, or not getting along with a teacher. This book will cover the myriad causes of school anxiety.

The Short- and Long-Term Effects of School Anxiety

Children with severe school anxiety are unlikely to outgrow it. However, the ways that anxiety manifests its effects can be damaging, making intervention and treatment essential to a child's health and well-being. Short-term effects of school anxiety include the following:

- Missing out on important schoolwork if frequent absences or school refusal occur, stunting intellectual development and creating a record of poor academic performance

- Not being able to relate well to peer group reduces social growth
- Potential increase in frustration levels, stress, and tension among family members

Long-term effects of school anxiety can include chronic anxiety or the development of an anxiety disorder, chronic underachievement in school, low self-esteem, and difficulties in achieving a satisfying personal and professional adulthood.

Why Is My Child Anxious?

The answer to why a child has anxiety is complex. There is no known single cause of anxiety and many experts believe it is caused by a combination of innate characteristics and external experiences, situations, and events.

Heredity

DNA is a personal blueprint, determining height, hair color, body type, and innate talents. Even a person's attitude about life, certain behaviors, emotional structure, and the degree of sensitivity to internal and external stimuli have been linked to genetics through years of research. Anxiety and many related disorders seem to run in families.

Biology

The physical and mental manifestations of anxiety create an intense arousal to real or perceived dangers. The nervous system, which includes the brain, spinal cord, organs, nerves, and chemicals in the body, produces these symptoms and emotions. Many experts believe that people who experience high arousal to perceived danger have a malfunction in brain chemicals that send messages throughout the body telling it that there is real danger that needs to be responded to even when there is no actual threat.

Personality Type

The intrinsic qualities and characteristics that include beliefs, attitudes, thoughts, emotions, habits, and behaviors make up personality. How these biological, psychological, and sociological factors combine in a unique way as a personality continues to tantalize researchers. Children who experience a high degree of anxiety seem to share many of the same personality traits and characteristics, which include:

- Greater degree of creativity and imagination; may have vivid mental images of himself in scary or terrifying situations leading to worry about the future; finds it difficult if not impossible to turn off these images.
- Difficulty in or fear of expressing feelings because others may get angry, or fear of losing control of emotions.
- Rigid thinking, for example, life is black or white, right or wrong; may be inflexible and unforgiving toward self and others.
- Perfectionism—a setup for failure and anxiety because of the attempt to achieve unrealistic goals and the focus on minor mistakes and flaws instead of seeing the positive side of things.

Other personal characteristics associated with anxiety include having an excessive need for acceptance and approval from others to feel worthwhile; being extremely sensitive to criticism; comparing oneself negatively to others; and being unaware of or ignoring a high degree of stress to the point where anxiety manifests itself in other ways, for example, as a feeling of physical illness.

Childhood and Family Factors

Mental health experts agree that childhood experiences, including the parents' style of parenting, combine with the child's innate qualities, such as the child's degree of emotional sensitivity, in the development of anxiety disorders.

It is not uncommon for parents to blame themselves for their child's anxiety. Maybe a parent is anxious and feels the child has learned to be anxious or is overly sensitive because of hereditary factors. Some parents blame themselves for feeling helpless to stop their child's suffering. Perhaps you blame yourself for your child's school anxiety. If so, remember that being a parent is a difficult job—and we spend quite a bit of it flying by the seat of our pants, trying to figure out what is best for our child. This book is not about blame; it is about teaching you, the parent, how to help your child make changes that will lead to the development of good life-coping skills, a sense of confidence and capability, and a reduction in or end to school anxiety.

Suggested changes are provided at the end of each chapter and include taking a look at your household and the environment in which your child lives; deciding what aspects of it, if any, are contributing to your child's anxiety; and then following guidelines on what to do to change things to help your child. For example, if you are a highly stressed and anxious parent, you can learn how to de-stress and relax yourself, and then teach your anxious child how to calm himself too. If you are overprotective of your child, you can learn that instead of rescuing him all the time, you can work on teaching him how to solve problems, make decisions, and learn how to face his fear, so that his self-confidence will grow.

Learning, Physical, and Emotional Disabilities

Disabilities such as learning disorders, attention-deficit/hyperactivity disorder (ADHD), autism, and cerebral palsy are likely to cause academic and social struggles, which can lead to feelings of being stupid and lazy and to being isolated by peers.

Medications

Medications such as over-the-counter antihistamines or cold remedies may cause anxiety in sensitive children. Caffeine found in sodas or the sports drinks targeted to elementary school athletes is closely associated with anxiety, as is nicotine.

Significant Life Events/Traumatic Events

Major life events have an impact on how children feel and behave. Big changes often lead to anxiety, such as a move to a new school, the death of a parent, or a parent leaving for military duty, making it difficult for children to function in school without distress. Traumatic events, such as physical and sexual attacks, leave children feeling vulnerable and helpless and may lead to stress disorders that can have a negative impact on their ability to function well in the learning environment.

戉戉

There are many resources available to help your child overcome school anxiety, which are discussed in this book. You will read about stress and why anxiety develops, and what exactly your child is experiencing when she is crying and begging you to let her stay home. Several chapters discuss in detail specific types of anxiety such as separation anxiety disorder, social anxiety, panic attacks, and the avoidance of situations. Also included are chapters on the anxiety produced by the demands of school, such as testing, doing homework, and dealing with bullies. Later in the book are chapters that have step-by-step instructions on how to teach your child to ease anxiety and take control of his anxiety instead of having it control him. These include the use of breathing, mental visualization, role playing, taking mock tests at home, and other techniques for overcoming school anxiety.

If your child has school anxiety, you have probably experienced a range of emotions from worry to frustration, maybe anger, and even downright fear about how your child is feeling and behaving and trying to figure out what in the world you can do about it. The book you hold in your hands contains information and a holistically oriented program that can assist you in helping your child become a successful, happy student.

CHAPTER 2

Anxiety Is a Mind-Body Experience

෨෨

MOST ELEMENTARY SCHOOL CHILDREN WITH SCHOOL ANXIETY cannot make sense of their anxious symptoms; they just know that they feel nervous, get physically sick, or just don't want to go to school. Many children are outwardly anxious and panicky on school mornings, like Sean, who can't stop himself from screaming to stay home and shaking all the way to school. Some children may not feel consciously anxious, but they still try to avoid school, like Tiara, who denies being anxious, but complains of a stomachache on most school mornings and sometimes throws up on test days. Other children fear their symptoms are caused by a disease, like Jaime, who believes that the heart palpitations he has in school are due to a bad heart and that he might die. No matter the reason for school anxiety or how it manifests, children who have it do suffer.

When children become anxious, they are not just feeling nervous; in fact every aspect of their physical, mental, and emotional functioning is affected. Symptoms can vary from feeling out of control and scared when walking through the school doors every morning to being unable to remember what was studied for a test to shaking and being unable to answer when called on in class.

School is a tension-filled environment with stressors that include leaving the safety of home to go to school, being judged and evaluated by teachers, fitting in with peers, or being bullied. Stressors are events, circumstances, or situations that create physical or emotional strain, frustration, and pressure. Some stressors are considered negative, for example, if a child has trouble reading and is failing second grade. However, stress is also felt around positive situations, such as a student soloing in the spring concert and feeling the pressure to play perfectly.

Anxiety is one type of a response to stress. The way children react to stress is determined by a number of factors, such as heredity, learned behaviors, life experiences, physical and mental health, and the number of stressors that are occurring all at once. Positive ways to handle stress can be learned, so teaching your school-anxious child how to cope with and adapt to stressful situations will reduce anxiety and make for a more positive school experience.

As a parent of a child with school anxiety, you know how difficult it can sometimes be to understand your child's behaviors, and how upsetting it is to watch her struggle. If you had school anxiety yourself, you can probably understand your child's experience. Parents often ask, "Why does my child feel that going to school is a jail sentence?" "Why are my child's symptoms so intense?" "Why can't my child think anxiety away?" These are important questions to have answered, and the first step in helping your child is to understand why and how the disturbing symptoms are created and how chronic school anxiety develops.

What Is the Nervous System?

The symptoms of anxiety are created by a primitive defense mechanism called the fight-or-flight response. This response is the body's way of protecting itself in situations that could result in injury or death. Every living thing on earth has a fight-or-flight response, from the one-cell amoeba to the human body, which is made up of trillions of cells. This defense is a function of the nervous system, which includes the brain, spinal cord, and other structures. The nervous system coordinates all life functions, including breathing, limb movement, organ action, thinking, feelings, and emotions. It is really a communication system, and one of its main jobs is to alert the body to external situations and events and then to prepare an appropriate response to them. For example, you want to hug your child. Your brain sends this message to the nerve cells and chemicals that control your limbs, allowing you to put your arms around your child. Or, your child's ball rolls into the street and without thinking she starts to run after it. In a split second, stress hormones course throughout your body, you yell at her to stop, but she doesn't hear you. Your respiration revs up, and nerve cells send messages to your legs enabling you to run like an Olympian to stop her. Whether it is giving your child a hug or running after her, all of this activity occurs in seconds without conscious thought.

The Fight-or-Flight Response

The fight-or-flight response is an alarm system located in a nervous system called the sympathetic nervous system. It jump-starts when real physical danger is present, but it will also activate if a situation is perceived or thought of as being threatening. For an example of a real danger, let's say your child is in the school yard playing with his friends when the school bully comes over with a group of followers. The bully begins to taunt your child and make threatening movements that he is going to hit him. Your child's fight-or-flight response kicks in to help him defend himself by either running away or trying to fight back.

For an example of a perceived danger situation, let's say your child has test anxiety. The night before a test she tries to study but feels sick to her stomach and later can't fall asleep. On the day of the test, her heart beats fast and she is irritable with a feeling of dread. Her anxiety spikes when the test is passed out to the children and the fight-or-flight response revs up to defend her from what she believes to be a dangerous situation. She has panic symptoms that make it hard for her to concentrate and do well. Of course, a test is not really dangerous, but when your child sees it as a threat, then the brain cannot distinguish between real or perceived danger and will protect her in either case.

What Happens to My Child During the Fight-or-Flight Response?

When danger is sensed, the brain immediately sends messages to the sympathetic nervous system to begin the defense, and powerful physiological changes take place all at once. These changes, which create the symptoms associated with anxiety, can be disturbing and frightening. Your child might experience the following physical symptoms from school anxiety:

- Pounding, rapid heartbeat or palpitations from the increase in blood pressure when stress hormones, such as adrenaline and cortisol, are released into the bloodstream, thereby pumping more blood into the brain, muscles, and other organs. At the same time, blood flow decreases to extremities, so hands and feet feel cold.
- Rapid breathing, which increases oxygen levels. However, shallow breathing may occur too, causing shortness of breath, gasping, and hyperventilation, often associated with feeling trapped and leads to sensations of being smothered. Hyperventilation is abnormal deep breathing that reduces levels of carbon dioxide in the blood, causing tingling in fingers, dizziness, and fainting.
- Tension in muscles as they ready themselves for action, which may create body and chest pain, leading to fears of a disease or heart attack, and numbness in the face, head, and limbs.
- Sweating as the body cools itself to prepare for physically demanding activity, either battle or flight. Sometimes a hot flush, blush, or chills are felt, too.
- Vision changes when pupils dilate to let in more light to increase awareness of the environment and the danger, sometimes creating hypersensitivity to light and other visual stimuli, or distorted vision, such as tunnel vision.

Other physiological changes include a decrease in saliva production to stop digestion, creating dry mouth; voiding of bowel and bladder to empty the body for action, leading to frequent urination and diarrhea; headaches because of muscle tension in the head, neck, and shoulders; hypersensitive nerve endings affecting the delicate skin, causing feelings of numbness, rashes, hives, and other skin conditions. However, the physical symptoms are only the beginning; the emotional manifestations of anxiety pack a wallop, too.

Mental Symptoms of the Fight-or-Flight Response

The mental signs of anxiety play havoc with cognitive functions. Thought processes become distorted, making it extremely difficult to think clearly and rationally. The ability to focus and concentrate decreases, which makes learning new material difficult. Other common emotions include feeling:

- Overwhelmed and out of control
- Helpless, hopeless, and wanting to flee the situation
- Irritable and angry
- Embarrassed and ashamed

Some children feel mild electrical shocks throughout their bodies when anxiety is high, due to sensitized nerve impulses. They may feel disconnected or dissociated from their own mind and body or may be jittery and unable to sit still. Others feel physically off balance, and even think they are going crazy. Anxiety and its distressing symptoms generally do not remain at high levels for more than ten minutes at a time, although symptoms can spike up and down for hours. Fortunately, the body also has a cool-down phase.

The Relaxation Response

After the threat or danger has passed, the parasympathetic nervous system is set in motion, decreasing stress hormones, returning blood pressure and respiration to normal, ramping up digestion, and relaxing major muscle groups. This a time of rest and renewal for the body. This branch of the nervous system is not an opposing force of the sympathetic nervous system; rather the two are complementary systems that work to ensure survival by trying to maintain a perfect balance in the body, called homeostasis. Anxiety affects every aspect of the mind and the body. It runs on a continuum, from mild to severe. However, even moderate symptoms can throw a child into a tizzy, making school the last place on earth a child wants to go to five days a week for most of the year.

For children who have school anxiety, it is very difficult to turn off the sympathetic response and turn on the parasympathetic state of calm because the majority of their lives is spent trying to navigate their fears about school. Long weekends and summer vacation can't erase having to cope with nine months of feeling distressed and nervous. For these children, school anxiety becomes a recurrent condition, but the good news is that it is possible to consciously create the relaxation response and decrease anxiety symptoms.

How Does School Anxiety Become Chronic?

School anxiety can easily become a chronic state unless some kind of intervention or treatment is provided. The cycle into a persistent state of anxiety looks like this:

Tiara, a nine-year-old fourth grader, generally liked school, but by second grade she began to experience panic. When she was called on to answer an arithmetic question or go to the board to work on a problem, she would get very nervous and not be able to think.

Since second grade, after many experiences of not knowing the answer or being stumped at the board and having classmates tease her about it, Tiara feels stupid and is nervous about going to school. Now, when she is called on for a math answer, the fight-or-flight response kicks in immediately. Her heart pounds, her whole body tenses, she feels unable to catch her breath, and if her anxiety spikes higher, she may experience that scary feeling she's told her parents about, when she feels distanced from the class and can't hear the teacher. This severe anxious reaction makes it impossible for Tiara to think clearly and come up with the correct response to a math problem she does know the answer to or to learn how to work out problems she doesn't understand.

When math class is over or when she's on her way home from school, the parasympathetic nervous system activates to return Tiara's body into a less aroused state and a more relaxed one. However, her relaxed state never reaches its normal resting condition because tomorrow school looms and the worry about math is never more than a few days away. The cycle of Tiara's chronic anxiety is caused by her thoughts about past classroom experiences where she felt humiliated, and the worry that these same situations and her feelings about them will occur again in the future.

The fight-or-flight reaction is a wonderful defense system; after all it has allowed humans to survive to this day. However, its intended purpose is to act as a short-term solution to a physical threat, not as a continuous state of mind and body. A chronically anxious child, whose fight-or-flight reaction is always just below the surface, will not be able to decrease stress hormones or other anxiety symptoms to normal healthy levels, interfering with the body's balance and functioning. If not treated, a child may develop an anxiety disorder, such as a panic disorder or phobias. Along with anxiety, other ailments can develop such as depression, avoidance of challenging situations, eating and sleeping problems, or a depressed immune system.

Explaining the Fight-or-Flight Response to Your Child

Find time when you will not be rushed. Tell your child your concerns about what you see regarding her symptoms, behavior, and school performance. Read the lists of fight-or-flight symptoms on pages 13 and 14 and have her check off those she experiences. Even if she denies being anxious, continue explaining. Say that the fight-or-flight response is her brain setting off a false alarm when it thinks there is danger. Give her an example of real physical danger. For example, she's walking in a park when all of a sudden someone on a bicycle veers toward her. In an instant, her brain sends the message to her legs, "Jump out of the way!" And she does. Next, show a false alarm by setting off a smoke detector. Say, "See, there is no fire, but the alarm does not know that. It's the same with your brain. It does not know that there is no real physical danger, such as when you are anxious about taking a test. So, the brain sends out messages to all parts of your body to get ready to keep you safe. Test taking is not really harmful, but you fear it, so the brain is confused." Make sure she understands this concept and tell her that with your help she is going to learn how to tell her brain that there is no danger and keep the false alarm from happening.

Is My Child Under Stress?

Children who are under stress often have a hard time talking about what is troubling them, so it is through behavior that stress is most likely revealed. Sometimes signs of stress are visible, but look for subtle signs, too. If you think something is "off" with your child, it probably is. Signs of stress include the following:

- Not wanting to leave parents or the house to go to school
- Having changes in mood, such as irritability, depression, or anxiety
- Being easily angered; engaging in aggressive behaviors, such as yelling, hitting, kicking, and biting
- Withdrawing socially from friends and activities
- Having crying spells, sadness, or lethargy
- Having problems in forming good teacher/student or student/student relationships

Other indicators include refusing to do homework or participate in class or school activities; trouble concentrating in school; drop in grades; problems sleeping or nightmares; loss of appetite or overeating; whining; physical complaints such as headaches, stomachaches, or body aches; biting fingernails; or pulling out hair. If any of these symptoms or behaviors persist, take your child to your family doctor and also see a mental health specialist. Children do not live in a vacuum; they live in a family, modeling their behavior after their parents and feeding off the family tension. To help your child to de-stress and learn how to cope with stressful situations, you need to assess the stress level in your family environment.

Is My Family Environment Stressful?

Take a long, hard look at your own stress and that of other family members. If stress levels are high, begin to de-stress by talking with your partner about what changes have to be made. Then include other children and family members in the conversation.

Evaluate your own stress management skills and that of other adults in the household. Be honest about how you handle what life throws at you. Do you tend to panic, get angry, feel helpless, or argue with your partner? What do school mornings look like? Are they chaotic and tense? Filled with yelling and rushing to get to the bus? What happens when your child balks at doing homework? Are you frustrated or annoyed? Are you overworked and find it hard to spend time with your child and family? Do family members make time to talk to each other about the day's events or their feelings? Is there lots of arguing among family members? Has there been a major change in the family such as moving, new baby, divorce, death, or financial difficulties? If you answered yes to even a few of these questions, then changing family dynamics is necessary to help your child conquer anxiety and succeed in school. What follows are suggestions for helping your child cope with stress.

How to Make Going to School Less Stressful

School mornings can be chaotic and anxiety filled with the pressure of getting children off to school and adults to work. The following suggestions can help to ease the pressure of the morning rush. The night before school have your child start homework or studying early, when he is not tired and you have time to check over his work or help him, and sign any forms that have to be returned to school. This way he'll feel prepared to go to school in the morning. Pack book bags, lay out clothes, and make lunches. Allow for playtime and family time before his bedtime. Get him to bed on time. In the morning, wake your child early enough so he can eat breakfast and get ready for school without rushing, maybe spend time with you or other family members, and catch the bus on time.

How to Help Your Child Cope with Stress

First, learn how to handle stress in healthy ways so you can model good coping skills. Learn how to breathe, relax, and deal with life situations in productive and proactive ways. Explain the dynamics of stress to your child, and help him become aware of the early signs. Teach your child the skills to handle stress by listening when he talks about how he feels, and not judging him. Help build his confidence by problem solving with him; don't always tell him what to do. Besides love and praise, provide structure, support, rules, and limits, so he feels cared for and safe. Have fun with him and make spending family time together a priority in your household.

CHAPTER 3

Help! My Child Won't Go to School

‿

MANY CHILDREN FROM KINDERGARTEN ON EXPERIENCE ANXIety when they are faced with the reality of going to school and leaving the safety of their home. The reasons for separation anxiety can range from a diagnosed anxiety disorder, to having turmoil at home, to being bullied in school, to having a learning disability. No matter the reason, school refusal or school avoidance causes pain and suffering for the child and her family, stress for school personnel, and both short- and long-term negative effects on the child's life.

Tony is in kindergarten. He went to a preschool where his mother worked as a teacher's aide and enjoyed his experience there. However, the night before his first day of kindergarten, he woke several times with nightmares. The morning of the first day of kindergarten, Tony said he did not want to go to school. He began crying and begging his mother to keep him at home. When she tried to put him on the school bus, he clung to her leg and wouldn't let go. Now, every morning is a nightmare trying to get Tony to school and the whole family is tense about it.

Sarah is in sixth grade. She is quiet and shy and was a good student up until this year. Sarah had two best friends from kindergarten to fifth grade. However, her friends are in a different class this year and have begun excluding Sarah. They don't invite her to hang out with them, and they have snubbed her in the lunchroom. Sarah feels devastated. By the second month of school, Sarah began complaining of severe cramps and stomach problems that usually begin on Sunday evenings and also occur most school mornings, when she begs her mother to keep her home. She has frequent absences and often leaves class and goes to the nurse's office. She is behind in most of her subjects.

Derek is a fourth grader. He balks about going to school and it's a fight to get him out of bed and dressed in the morning. Derek has a history of anxiety and schoolwork has always been a challenge for him. He tests poorly on most subjects and his grades are below average. The morning of a test, Derek gets sick to his stomach and usually throws up his breakfast and begs his mother to keep him home. Right before a test, Derek's heart begins to race and he feels like he can't catch his breath. When his test paper is in front of him, he can't remember what he studied. Sometimes, he puts his name on the paper and nothing else. During the last math test, his writing hand tingled and then went numb. His parents are worn down by the fight and are thinking of putting him on homebound study, where teachers from his school will come to his house to teach, give assignments, and test him for the rest of the year.

This chapter discusses school refusal, the reasons children fight to stay home, and includes guidelines and exercises to help your child get off to school with less fuss, making a positive change for your child, yourself, and your family.

Why Is Separating So Hard to Do?

At about eight months of age, your baby most likely went through periods of distress when he was separated from you. Before that age, he probably did not cry when you left his line of vision, because his brain was not developed enough to recognize that you still existed even though you were no longer in his sight. To his level of understanding, "out of sight" meant "out of mind."

But sometime between eight and nine months of age, you noticed that he became agitated if he could not see you. Or perhaps he cried when you allowed someone unfamiliar to hold him. This change in your baby's behavior is due to a cognitive developmental shift called object permanence, which was first identified by Jean Piaget, a Swiss psychologist. It is your baby's ability to understand that you exist even when he can't see you. At this stage in his development, your baby was able to retain a mental image of you when you left him, and he missed you. Revised theories state that babies as young as three months old may develop object permanence.

During childhood development, children between the ages of eighteen and twenty-four months often have periods of separation anxiety, too. When your child was a toddler, she may have cried and clung to you if you were leaving her with a babysitter or in day care. Although difficult to cope with, separation anxiety is considered normal at certain childhood developmental stages.

However, separation anxiety may occur in other developmental stages as well. As your child grows and goes out into the world, major transitions such as going to school for the first time or entering middle school can create distress for your child, causing her to become anxious when she is away from you and the safety of her home. Feelings of anxiety around these changes are normal.

Tony from our opening case illustrates what makes separating from parents and home so distressing. Tony always felt safe and protected with his mother at home or in preschool. However, going to school without his mother meant leaving his comfort zone. In kindergarten, he was faced for the first time with having to handle things alone. He worried, "What if the kids in class aren't nice or don't like me? What if my teacher is mean? What if the work is too hard?"

Children in kindergarten have to meet the expectations of adults they don't know and try to make friends with other students who are strangers. They are also being evaluated, graded, and judged in comparison to their peers, and that can be intimidating. These new experiences have to be handled without the safety of parents and home. No wonder children have separation anxiety. Most children adjust in a few weeks, but if they don't and the anxiety persists, an anxiety disorder could develop. Major changes such as losing the support of friends, or school problems such as learning disabilities, create stress and can make school an unhappy place for a child.

What Is School Refusal?

At one time, school avoidance was inaccurately called school phobia because many children who have difficulty attending school are not afraid of school but may be troubled due to other reasons such as bullying and problems at home. The terms currently used by educators and mental health specialists are either *school refusal* or *school avoidance*. Maybe you have a child who is fighting tooth and nail to stay home on a school day. Or perhaps he goes to school under duress but has trouble staying there and frequents the nurse's office, calling you to come and get him. You are probably worried and frustrated and are at your wit's end about what to do. The following section identifies the hallmarks of school refusal.

What Are the Signs of School Refusal/School Avoidance?

School refusal is not a diagnosable condition like separation anxiety disorder, which is a formal mental condition. School refusal only refers to the behavior of the child, but it is considered a serious emotional problem. If your child does everything she can to avoid going to school, she may exhibit a number of the following physical symptoms:

- Dizziness
- Shakiness or trembling
- Rapid heartbeat, chest pains, or hyperventilation
- Sweating
- Headaches
- Stomachaches, vomiting, or diarrhea
- Panic attacks

Your child may cry and beg you to keep her home, have tantrums, exhibit anger, feel sad and depressed, have insomnia, and be unable to concentrate. If your child's symptoms become severe, she may threaten to harm herself if she has to go to school. She may be impossible to wake in the morning, chronically miss the bus, be unable to stay in school if she does go, and avoid social contact with peers. Many children go to school without protesting but suffer in silence, feeling trapped and miserable throughout the day.

If your child has school avoidance, he may also worry about missing schoolwork and try his best to keep up with his studies. If he is allowed to stay at home, where he feels safe, he probably feels guilty and remorseful about creating turmoil in the family. Your child is not alone in wanting to avoid school, for research indicates that as many as one in four children will exhibit school avoidance at some time during their school years from kindergarten through twelfth grade.

School refusal may begin when your child first enters kindergarten or even nursery school and lessen or worsen over time. Sometimes, your child may grudgingly go to school each day, but symptoms may worsen if he has been home for an extended period of time due to an illness or a vacation. Sunday nights are commonly difficult for children who have school refusal; they often begin complaining of stomachaches or other ills after being home for the weekend.

School Refusal Is Not Truancy

Your child is not a truant if he suffers from school refusal. School refusal is an emotional condition and differs from truancy, a delinquency problem usually seen in teens, but can start by sixth grade. Children who are truant intentionally choose not to attend school, and they may not stay home when they cut school. A truant child usually does not experience the anxiety, worry, or guilt about not attending school. This child will lie to his parents about being absent and begin to exhibit delinquent and antisocial behaviors, such as stealing and using drugs. Truant children ordinarily have no interest in schoolwork and do not conform to academic and behavioral standards and expectations.

What Is Separation Anxiety Disorder?

Anxiety about being separated from parents or primary caregivers is a healthy normal response for children from infancy to about age four, as well as during the child's major growth transitions such as going from home life into school. The distress felt by the child is usually eased by comforting him or refocusing his attention. Eventually, as he adapts to the change, his symptoms and behaviors stop and he is able to adjust into his new role as a student. If your child's separation anxiety symptoms persist beyond the normal developmental stage or increase in severity, he may be developing separation anxiety disorder (SAD), which is a major reason for school refusal.

SAD is one of eleven anxiety disorders listed in the DSM-IV, the *Diagnostic and Statistical Manual of Mental Disorders,* 4th ed., used by mental health professionals for diagnostic purposes and to help create a treatment plan. SAD is a common disorder and its impact goes way beyond the behaviors seen in school refusal. Avoiding school at any cost is a major issue for children with SAD. In order for your child to be diagnosed with SAD, he must meet the following criteria:

- Experiences excessive anxiety if he anticipates leaving parents or home
- Fears that a disaster or death will occur when away from parents or home
- Fears or refuses to go to school or be away from home or parents
- Is afraid to sleep alone without parents near
- Has recurring nightmares about being separated from parents or home

Children with SAD may also experience and exhibit symptoms and behaviors that include panic attacks; fears about monsters, animals, or having the house broken into; fear of being alone in a room; or fear of the dark. Another clue to SAD is a child's distress over or refusal to participate in school trips or sleepovers at friends' or family members' homes. Any situation that causes a child discomfort may bring on crying and clinging, tantrums, stomachaches, diarrhea, vomiting, headaches, shakiness, or numbness and tingling in the hands and legs. The child may also exhibit extreme stress in social situations with peers and do poorly academically.

Avoidance

An important characteristic of both school refusal and separation anxiety disorder is that anxiety and reluctance to go to school will increase if the child is allowed to stay home. The more a child is able to avoid school, the more difficult it will be to return to school. When a child is able to avoid the anxious situation, anxiety lessens, thereby reinforcing that staying home feels better. Who can blame a child for wanting to feel better? If your child's symptoms continue for more than two weeks, meet with her teacher and guidance counselor to find out if anything in school is creating the anxiety and to problem solve with them. If the symptoms still persist, take your child to your family physician to rule out a medical condition, and if necessary contact a mental health specialist.

The Short- and Long-Term Effects of School Refusal and SAD

Whether your child exhibits school refusal or separation anxiety disorder, treatment is crucial to prevent negative psychological, social, and academic consequences to your child, yourself, and your family. The short-term impact on your child includes a high degree of stress and anxiety, poor academic performance, and isolation from peers. Turmoil, tension, and conflict will likely be high for other family members.

Studies by the National Institute of Mental Health (NIMH) and other institutions show that without treatment the long-term effects continue throughout the life span. Children with school refusal or SAD have a high risk of developing other mental conditions such as depression and other anxiety disorders such as social anxiety disorder. The usage of alcohol and drugs is higher in children who avoid school and this usage may continue into adulthood. Other long-term consequences include a high risk of dropping out of high school, a higher percentage requiring outpatient or inpatient psychiatric care, and a high risk of participating in criminal behavior. A child who suffers from school anxiety may be unable to become an independent adult who can lead a rich and fulfilling life. He may be stuck in dead-end jobs and be at a high risk of having problems in interpersonal relationships and getting a divorce.

What Are the Effects of School Refusal on the Family?

The effects of school anxiety on you and your family can be difficult to cope with. It is gut-wrenching to watch your child suffer, but you may also feel afraid, frustrated, disappointed, resentful, annoyed, angry, and worn out. If your child has school refusal or SAD, she requires a large amount of your time and attention with her constant need for reassurance, your having to deal with her tantrums, and the daily fight to get her to go to school. If you have other children, they may feel resentful or ashamed of their sibling's behavior. You and your spouse or partner may argue about what to do for your child and even blame each other. Finding out how to help your child or getting professional help will benefit your entire family.

Why Does My Child Refuse to Go to School?

School refusal is a complex condition and may be caused by a combination of psychological, biological, and sociological factors that make it difficult to answer the question, "Why does my child refuse to go to school?" There are numerous reasons for your child's reluctance including temperament (innate characteristics that are a part of personality), an anxiety disorder, family functioning, changes in the family, problems in the school environment such as bullying, and traumatic experiences and events.

Overcoming School Refusal Clinic

If your child is chronically fighting you about going to school, your reaction and the way your family members and other adults respond will positively or negatively impact your child's stress levels, anxiety, adjustment to school, and treatment. The following information will enable you to help your child ease anxiety, increase coping skills, and build confidence.

✎ Guidelines for Helping Your Child with School Refusal

1. Listen to your child and acknowledge her feelings no matter how irrational they sound. Say things like, "I know you are worried that something will happen to me when you are in school" or "I know you are afraid you'll blank out during the math test." Do not say, "That's silly, there's nothing to be afraid of."

2. Reassure and comfort your child. Say things like, "I know you are afraid, but nothing will happen to me" or "I know you'll do your best." Let him know that you are there to help him conquer his anxiety. He is not alone.

3. Never make fun of, ridicule, scream at, punish, or demean your child because of his fears. Do not allow family members or other adults to do so either. Always encourage your child to come to you with any worries or fears he may have.

4. Be aware of your own anxiety and worry about your child when you are around her. If you show how upset you are about what is happening, you'll increase her anxiety. Believe in your child's capacity to overcome her anxiety and succeed and let your child know that you believe in her.

5. Contact your child's school to see if anything is happening there that is creating school avoidance, for example, problems with a teacher, your child's inability to understand the work, or bullying or other forms of violence.

6. Talk to your child without anger about why he must go to school—to learn, make friends, it's the law, and so forth.
7. Ask your child for her input in solving the problem. Partnering with your child instead of trying to "rescue" her will make her feel more in control of the situation and help build her confidence.
8. Take stock of your morning routine. Is it anxiety-filled with tension, rushing, and yelling to get everyone out the door? If so, make changes that will reduce the stress.
9. Model good stress management and life-coping skills. Learn how to defuse your anxiety by using techniques for relaxing and teach them to your child and family.

Exercises

Sending your school-anxious child off to school without giving her the tools to cope with the intense emotions created by school anxiety is like sending her off in a boat without a paddle. The following exercises and techniques will help her get to school by teaching her to take control of her anxiety instead of having it control her. The following groups of exercises are prerequisites: Breathing (Chapter 14), Staying in the Moment (Chapter 15), Facing Fear (Chapter 16), and Systematic Desensitization (Chapter 5). Read through the book for additional exercises that can be adapted to the problem of school refusal.

GOING TO SCHOOL STEP-BY-STEP

Tell your child that you are going to help her go to school by having her imagine going to school one step at a time when she is relaxed. Now create with her a hierarchy of fears about going to school by reading the exercises in Chapter 5. Next, have your child lie down or sit in a comfortable chair and adapt the desensitization exercise to meet her needs. For example, step one: after waking up on a school morning, breathe and be calm; step two: get out of bed; step three: get dressed; and so on until your child imagines walking into school and going to class while relaxed. If need be, create two hierarchies, one for going through the school doors, the other for being in class, doing class work, taking tests, and so forth. Practice every night running through the whole hierarchy or hierarchies at least twice. With time, your child will be able to take control of herself in the real situation.

ADDITIONAL TIPS FOR EASING LEAVING HOME FOR SCHOOL

Kindergarten children have to adjust to a whole new way of life, leaving home for a good part of the day, every school day for the next nine months. Some children have anxiety for the first weeks, even months, every time a new school year begins. Here are some suggestions that should help: Tell your child what to expect in school about the work, recess, and so forth. Visit the school before it starts if possible, walk around the halls, go into his classroom, and meet the teacher. Let him take a favorite toy, photo, or object that signifies home (older children may do this, too). With permission in the lower grades, stay in the classroom with him for a short period of time. Always pick him up on time at school or the bus stop. Leave your child with trusted sitters so he can get used to you being away and never make a fuss about leaving him; kiss him quickly and walk away. Teach your child good coping skills and to be self-reliant by encouraging independent play. Get professional help immediately if school refusal persists.

Whether your child has school refusal or has been diagnosed with an anxiety disorder, he is stressed out every day, which is affecting him physically and emotionally. If school refusal is chronic and severe, he will feel isolated from his classmates and may even be teased about his behavior if other students realize what is happening. The good news is that anxiety can be overcome with patience and encouragement by engaging your child in the healing process.

CHAPTER 4

My Child Can't Stop Worrying

ᑫ

W E ALL WORRY. WORRY IS NORMAL; EXCESSIVE WORRY IS not. Children often worry about school, for example, about starting a new school year, making friends, doing homework, getting good grades, or leaving the safety of home. Children also bring their worries from home into school, such as being jealous toward a new baby in the family, living in a chaotic home environment, or dealing with parental divorce.

Sometimes, worry can be a positive motivating force for taking action or making behavioral changes.

Kamal realized on the way to school that he had forgotten his spelling homework. He worried all the way to school about what his teacher would do when she found out. So, the next morning before he left for school he double-checked his book bag for his spelling homework.

Sarah was mean to her friends, so they avoided her during recess. That night she worried that they wouldn't want to play with her anymore. The next day, she apologized and is more careful about how she behaves toward them.

Worry is generally short term, focused on a specific event or circumstance, and normally stops when the situation is resolved. For example, if a child has learning difficulties and worries about finishing his or her homework, that is normal worry for that situation. If help is beneficial, the worry should cease. But a child who worries all the time is unable to function normally and happily at home, in school, and with peers. Without intervention and treatment, chronic worry could have long-lasting effects into adulthood.

Chronic Worry

An integral component of anxiety is worry. A child who is a continual worrier will obsess about past and present experiences and feel anxious about what might happen in the future.

> *Maria, a six-year-old first grader, has her parents very concerned because they say, "She worries all the time about everything." Her worries include being afraid to leave home because something bad might happen to her mother, as well as every school morning being terrified that she'll miss the bus and be late for school. If her mother drives her to school, Maria is afraid they'll run out of gas. At night, she imagines that her teacher was mad at her that day, although nothing occurred in class. Maria fears that she will get hurt when she plays outside, so she avoids recess and tells her friends to "be careful" when they play.*
>
> *Maria is tense and jumpy all the time. Worry makes it impossible for her to have fun. When a worry begins, she repeats her concerns over and over again. She has trouble falling asleep and complains of frequent stomachaches. Often, she asks her mother if she can stay home from school. Poor grades reflect how difficult it is for her to concentrate in class or on tests, increasing her worry about school. Her parents try to reassure her but Maria cannot stop the continual worry.*

If you have a child whose symptoms and behaviors are similar to Maria's, she may have generalized anxiety disorder (GAD).

Generalized Anxiety Disorder

Generalized anxiety disorder affects children, adolescents, and adults. It is defined as persistent and excessive worry about situations and events. Apprehension about future happenings is a key sign of the disorder, but anxiety occurs around past and present situations, too. The word *generalized* describes how pervasively and widespread the anxiety and distress is felt, impacting every aspect of the sufferer's life. If not treated, a child will likely suffer into adulthood. The level of anxiety fluctuates but spikes at stressful times. The National Institute of Mental Health (NIMH) indicates that of the more than 36 million children who attend elementary school, about a million will develop GAD.

Children have a hard time talking about their anxiety, and one aspect of generalized anxiety disorder that makes it very difficult for children to cope with is that their anxious feelings may not have an obvious cause. Often the anxiety is considered to be "free-floating," because symptoms seems to come out of the blue, for no reason. This feature of the disorder can create distress for the child and makes treatment complex.

Although GAD has general characteristics found in children, adolescents, and adults, there are differences in how children experience it, due to their stage of development. They often become fixated on their worries about disasters striking their family or obsessively second-guess their behavior in school or social situations. Most children with GAD are unaware that their anxiety is out of proportion to the situation—and if they do recognize it, they can't turn off the worry.

Read the following questions, and if your child's worries interfere with his or her daily functioning, contact your family physician and a mental health specialist.

✎ Does My Child Have Generalized Anxiety Disorder?

1. Does your child worry excessively most days about daily activities and school situations such as being on time, peer relationships, grades, or following school rules?

2. Does your child worry about her own safety or yours or that natural disasters, such as hurricanes, will injure or kill her or her family members?

3. Is your child apprehensive about new situations and does he obsess about the past?

4. Does your child require frequent approval from you, teachers, or other adults but cannot be reassured?

5. Is your child self-critical and does she express doubt about her abilities most of the time?

6. Is your child chronically anxious, on edge, and irritable?

7. Does your child complain of frequent headaches, stomachaches, exhaustion, and muscle tension?

8. Does your child have trouble falling or staying asleep?

9. Does your child find it difficult to concentrate, understand schoolwork, complete homework assignments, or test well due to worrying; or double- and triple-check schoolwork and other activities in an attempt to be "perfect"?

10. Does your child try to avoid school, beg to stay home, cry, or get sick at school?

11. Does your child try to avoid school activities, family outings, or playing with friends?

Other common symptoms include trembling and feeling shaky, being easily startled, needing to urinate frequently, experiencing nausea and diarrhea, sweating, having dry mouth or trouble swallowing, or feeling a lump in the throat.

I Think My Child Is Avoidant

Children who chronically worry or have GAD are at risk of becoming avoidant and of developing panic disorder with agoraphobia, which is the avoidance of people, places, and things that cause anxiety symptoms.

Daniel is a nine-year-old fourth grader. By second grade, he began to exhibit symptoms of GAD. One of his fears is that he will say the wrong thing in school, make a mistake, and feel embarrassed. When he does give a wrong answer in class, he can't stop himself from stammering and blushing. Some boys in his class picked up on his discomfort and tease him about it. Daniel doesn't just worry about what he could have said or done in class every day after school; he thinks about it, dwells on it, hour after hour, repeating the same scenario in his mind over and over to exhaustion. Now even the thought of answering in class is a nightmare for Daniel. He avoids answering any questions even if he knows the right answer, stopped participating in class, and has begun to avoid social interaction even with friends.

To a child who worries about his behavior, about what he does or says, and spends hours obsessing about past interactions with others believing he is being negatively evaluated and judged, avoidance seems like a good solution. Look at it from his point of view: If he puts himself in an anxious situation that he can't cope with, his anxiety spikes. When he leaves or avoids the situation, anxiety decreases and he feels better, thereby reinforcing the cycle of avoidance.

Long-Term Effects of GAD

Generalized anxiety disorder is distressing and debilitating to a child's well-being and increases the risk of developing other emotional disorders, such as depression, and anxiety disorders, such as social anxiety disorder (SAD) and obsessive-compulsive disorder (OCD). If a child has GAD and is not properly treated, there is a likelihood that the child will be unable to grow into an adult who can create a rich and satisfying life.

Causes of GAD

Generalized anxiety disorder is a complex condition for which a specific cause has not been found. Although a child may have inherited the tendency to react anxiously to life situations, most mental health experts believe that a combination of factors contributes to the condition's development, including the following:

1. *Heredity.* Genetics is thought to be a basis for GAD. It runs in some families, putting a child at risk if a parent has the disorder.

2. *Environment.* Children learn their fears, habits, attitudes, and ways of thinking about themselves and the world from watching how parents feel about themselves and act and react to others and the world around them. This is called modelling. Stressful or traumatic events such as abuse, parental divorce, death of a parent, or moving to a new school may also contribute to the development of GAD.

3. *Biology.* Some biological theories examine abnormal levels of the brain's neurotransmitters (serotonin and norepinephrine), while others speculate that parts of the brain that control emotions rev up the fight-or-flight response to meet a perceived danger and then can't shut down.

4. *Cognitive Behavior Theory.* This theory states that it is the individual's distorted view of perceived danger, along with a belief that he or she is unable to cope with or control the situation, that leads to anxiety symptoms. Psychoanalytic and psychodynamic theories look at an individual's buried or unresolved experiences and emotions as leading causes of anxiety.

The development of chronic worry or GAD seems to be a mix of a child's innate characteristics, tendencies, genetic makeup, experiences, attitudes, beliefs, and coping skills. It will take parental support, treatment, and even some life changes to enable a child to take control of the anxiety and to conquer it.

Available Treatments

The first step in treatment is to have your family physician perform a complete physical and to refer your child to a mental health specialist for an evaluation and possible psychological testing. Therapy is generally indicated for severe anxiety disorders and can include cognitive-behavioral therapy, behavioral therapy, psychotherapy, play therapy, and family therapy. A psychiatric evaluation may be recommended by your family physician or mental health practitioner.

Alternative treatments such as yoga and relaxation techniques, as well as dietary changes and getting your child involved in regular physical exercise, can aid in feelings of increased confidence in coping with stress and anxiety, and in your child feeling an overall sense of well-being. For detailed treatment information and the Overcoming School Anxiety Program suggestions, read Chapters 14 through 20. If you are considering the use of medication for your child, first educate yourself about the benefits and risks of medications by discussing them with your family doctor or therapist. Also, look for information at the library, in bookstores, and online.

Overcoming Chronic Worry and GAD Clinic

Being the parent of a child with generalized anxiety disorder can be exasperating, exhausting, and even frightening. Your child spins out of control and suffers with obsessive worry about mundane aspects of daily life, upsetting you and your entire family. Learning how to properly respond, communicate, and interact with your child, and helping her to improve her coping skills, will benefit your child and your family. The following guidelines and exercises can help you.

✎ Guidelines for Helping Your Child Cope with Worry and GAD

1. Do not yell at, punish, tease, or demean your child because of her anxiety or allow family members, friends, or others to do so.
2. Learn how to relax, yourself. If you are outwardly anxious around your child, about either her condition or anything else, it will feed her anxiety. Remember, your child not only learns how to cope from watching you but also takes cues from you about herself—if you are freaking out about her "illness," then she will too.
3. Teach your child how to relax. Even young children can be taught how to breathe properly and use other relaxation

techniques that will either ease or stop the fight-or-flight response from revving up.

4. Educate yourself. When you understand the nature of your child's anxiety, it will help you cope with her anxious symptoms and behaviors and also communicate effectively with the school and health professionals.

5. Communicate and listen. Children with anxiety know they are struggling, and often feel "different" and isolated from family and peers. Empathize with her feelings and allow her to talk without jumping in and trying to fix things.

6. Support and reassure. When your child has to face anxious situations, remind him that he has experienced stressful times before and "made it."

7. Problem solve with your child. Encouraging your child to engage in the process of overcoming chronic worry will increase her confidence and coping skills. For example, plan with her how to make school mornings less stressful.

If you are a chronic worrier or have GAD, you may want to tell your child you know how she feels, and even talk about some of the things you do to help you feel better. But be careful—too much detail or repetition about your own condition or what you have done to help yourself may upset your child or make her feel that she is not trying hard enough to overcome her own anxiety.

Also, become a good partner with your child's school by building a rapport with teachers, guidance counselors, and other school personnel. For example, if your child's worries make it difficult for him to stay all day in the classroom, work with his teacher to help him find a "safe place" as a respite until he can return to class.

Exercises

Chronically worried children have multiple concerns, and you can't work on all of them at one time. With your child, list all of his worries in your Overcoming School Anxiety Journal. Then, together decide which one to work on first. Only when he feels calmer and more confident about handling a worry should you move on to the next one. The following exercises will counter-condition your child to feel calm instead of anxious in certain situations, by pairing the worry with being in a relaxed state. Daily practice is the key to success. If your child is uncomfortable doing an exercise, don't force it. Stop the exercise and find another your child will engage in. Try again when your child is more confident, but remove the exercise from the program if he balks.

Prerequisites for the following exercises are learning how to belly breathe (Chapter 14), being able to stay in the moment (Chapter 15), and knowing how to let go of anxiety and float through it (Chapter 16).

"I'm Okay" with a Touch of a Finger

Explain to your child that in this exercise he is going to do belly breathing and at the same time touch his thumb and forefinger, making an "okay" sign. Demonstrate the okay sign to your child. Belly breathe by placing your hands on your belly below the bellybutton. When you inhale through your nose, your belly will expand; exhale through your nose, and your belly will relax. See Chapter 14 for details on learning how to belly breathe. Teach it to your child. Belly breathing is also effective for sleep problems. Chapter 14 contains an exercise that will help your child if he has trouble falling or staying asleep.

Tell your child that he is going to train himself how to relax quickly with the okay sign, and at the same time he will say to himself, "I'm okay." He can use this exercise in school situations or whenever his worry starts, and nobody will know he is doing it.

1. Have your child sit or lie down with his eyes closed and hands at his sides and belly breathe for a few minutes until he feels relaxed. Then have him stop belly breathing.
2. Using a watch with a second hand, have him belly breathe for thirty seconds while making the okay sign and saying to himself, "I'm okay." When thirty seconds is up, have him stop what he is doing and relax.

3. Repeat ten times.
4. Also have him practice with his eyes open and while standing and walking.

Ask your child if he likes this exercise and how he feels doing it. Practice in short spurts as often as possible to make the okay sign and relaxing second nature. An additional idea is to make a chart with your child listing where and when he will practice the "I'm okay" exercise, such as leaving home to go to school, in class, with classmates, and so forth. Leave spaces to check off completion of practice. If your family is stressed out, make the "I'm okay" exercise a fun family project, and if he wants to, have your child teach the exercise to family members.

IMAGINING WORRY

Tell your child that in this exercise you'll want him to imagine himself in a worrisome situation that may make him feel nervous while he is doing the exercise, but that he will belly breathe, relax himself, and therefore feel better. When the anxiety eases, he will say "time," stop the picture, and relax. Say that he is rehearsing how to feel good in situations that now make him feel bad. Have the School Anxiety Scale in Chapter 16 at hand. Together decide which worry your child should work on first.

1. Have your child sit in a chair or lie down and close his eyes.
2. Tell him to imagine the worry, to see himself in the situation and picture all the details that make him anxious. Ask him to rate his anxiety on the scale.
3. Now, while keeping the picture in his mind, have him begin belly breathing, continuing until he indicates that the anxiety has eased by saying "time." Have him rate his anxiety now on the anxiety scale.
4. Repeat five times. When the exercise is finished, have him relax and say how he feels. The goal of this exercise is to get your child to almost zero anxiety about a previously anxiety-producing situation.

Also practice the imagining worry exercise while doing the body awareness exercises in Chapter 15 and the loosening and floating exercises in Chapter 16.

∽

It is a difficult and slow process to conquer chronic worry and GAD. You have to expect days when your child will progress, and then days when he will seem to take a few steps back. The worry may come back with a vengeance even after it has been gone for some time. Explain to your child that this is normal to his healing and recovery. If it does come back, tell him, "No biggie, just a little practice will get things right again." You have to be patient. Reassure him that he is on the road to recovery, and praise him for his efforts in overcoming worry or generalized anxiety disorder.

CHAPTER 5

My Child Panics and Avoids Situations

∽

PANIC ATTACKS ARE ONE OF THE MOST DIFFICULT CONDITIONS to cope with, because the acute symptoms manifest in frightening ways. Having an attack in school is troublesome because symptoms can start anywhere, without warning, and the freedom to flee and find a safe place is not easy to do without explanation or embarrassment.

Since kindergarten, Rachel had separation anxiety every new school year, but her anxiety eased within the first few weeks and she was able to settle down and do well for the rest of the school year. But in fifth grade things changed. On a Monday morning after a long weekend, Rachel had her first panic attack when the teacher signaled that class was starting and closed the door. Suddenly, Rachel felt that she couldn't breathe. She was struck with the fear that she would suffocate and die. She could barely answer when the teacher called her name during attendance. Terrified, she wanted to run out of the classroom and go home to her mother, but she felt afraid that she would get in trouble and embarrass herself. After a few hours of suffering in silence, she told the teacher she was sick, went to the nurse, and her mother picked her up from school. At home her panic subsided, but the next morning, she had another attack just thinking about having the first attack and begged her mother to keep her home.

In this chapter you will learn about panic, its partner agoraphobia, the panic disorders, and their causes. Treatment options are discussed along with guidelines and exercises that will help your child learn how to overcome panic and avoidance.

What Are Panic Attacks?

A panic attack is a sudden surge of paralyzing fear that usually strikes for no apparent reason, although attacks can occur because of specific situations. Children who have panic attacks experience acute symptoms such as a pounding heartbeat, sweating, chest pain, numbness, or feelings of terror and helplessness. Children may not recognize the mental symptoms, but focus on the physical sensations of panic, such as a racing heart, stomachaches, dizziness, and trouble breathing. They may express their fears about having panic attacks by acting out with anger, aggression, avoidance, and hypochondria.

Vincent, a first grader, was sitting at a classroom table with three other students doing an art project when suddenly he felt a rush of adrenaline along with feelings of dread. He was terrified and began to visibly tremble and fidget in his seat. Vincent felt compelled to leave the class and run away. He raised his hand, but the teacher, working with other students, told him to wait a minute. When a classmate asked him what was wrong, Vincent lashed out and yelled, "Leave me alone!" then jumped out of his chair and headed for the door. When his teacher tried to stop him, he screamed at her and ran out.

Rachel and Vincent experience panic attacks, although their symptoms and behaviors differ. If the panic recurs without intervention and treatment, they have a good chance of developing panic disorder, which will curtail their lives and make them suffer.

Panic Attack Features and Symptoms

Panic attacks and panic disorders can begin anytime from childhood into late adulthood. Some children have one or two attacks but never have another one. Although children often experience and describe panic differently than adolescents and adults, the features of panic are universal. Most attacks begin and end within ten minutes, and others spike and lessen every few minutes, sometimes continuing for hours.

Spontaneous attacks are uncued. They come without warning and can strike even during relaxed times, for example, while your child is playing with friends, watching TV, or even waking from sleep. This is free-floating anxiety and creates the "the fear of the fear." With spontaneous attacks, it is the fear of the symptoms, not of a person, place, or thing, that causes the disorder. Cued attacks occur in specific situations, for example, while taking a test or in anticipation of a test.

Is My Child Having Panic Attacks?

Panic symptoms are so powerful and distressing that even young children can recall in some detail where they were and how sick and scared the attack made them feel. When panic strikes, it seems impossible to stop it or function normally during it. If your child has the following symptoms on a daily or weekly basis, contact your family physician and a mental health clinician.

- Rapid, pounding heartbeat and palpitations
- Hyperventilation, difficulty breathing, or chest pain
- Headache, dizziness, or light-headedness
- Stomachache, diarrhea, nausea, vomiting, or frequent urination
- Feelings of a coming dread or doom, that something horrible will happen
- Fears of being out of control, of being embarrassed or of going crazy
- Sweating, feeling clammy or chilled

In addition to the previous list of symptoms, does your child exhibit the following behaviors?

- Unrelenting worry about having a panic attack
- Chronic worry about experiencing the symptoms of panic

- School refusal or getting sick in school
- Avoidance of social situations, certain people, places, or things

Other symptoms include trembling and shakiness, tingling or numbness in the limbs, dry mouth, depression, and frightening distorted perceptions such as feeling disconnected from one's own body or having tunnel vision.

Think about what your child's mind and body are going through. The fight-or-flight response revs up ready for serious physical activity, the symptoms are frightening and confusing, and with no physical release of stress hormones, anxiety continues. If recurring panic attacks take place and avoidance becomes the main coping mechanism, then physical and mental exhaustion will follow. Avoidance leads to another aspect of panic—debilitating agoraphobia.

What Is Agoraphobia?

Agoraphobia develops when recurring panic attacks create severe apprehension about either having an attack or being trapped in a situation where an attack may occur but feeling there is no way to escape or to do so will cause embarrassment and humiliation. It is essentially the "fear of the fear" with avoidance generally as the first line of defense.

Casey, in sixth grade, began having severe panic attacks in school right after her father left home to fight in Iraq. During the first attack, she experienced tunnel vision where her sight blurred, peripheral vision darkened, and the front of the room looked like it was in a spotlight 100 miles away. Casey was paralyzed with fear and thought she was going blind. Subsequent medical tests proved normal and she was diagnosed with a severe stress reaction. Casey's panic attacks continued randomly at school, then spread to malls, the school bus, and anyplace where she feared being trapped. She only feels safe at home with her mother. Casey's anxi-

ety is so high at times, and she is so adamant about staying home, that the last time she missed the school bus, she tried to jump out of her mother's car on the way to school.

If your child has panic attacks, there is no certainty that agoraphobia will develop. But if it does, her world would shrink in relationship to the severity of her symptoms and coping skills. The development of a full-blown panic disorder can persist into adulthood, causing lifelong problems.

What Are the Panic Disorders?

There are three types of panic disorders, and although the differences are slight, the prescribed treatments may vary. Panic disorder without agoraphobia is recurring panic attacks, and the worry about future attacks, without avoidance of anxious situations or events. Panic disorder with agoraphobia is a pervasive avoidance of places where an attack might occur. Agoraphobia without history of panic disorder develops when the fear of having a panic attack is present even though an attack has never taken place or the ones that did occur were mild in nature. This condition most likely develops because avoidance begins almost immediately, with the first symptoms.

Although a diagnosis of panic disorder must meet clinical standards, panic is a unique experience and varies in its course and effects on each child it touches. The intensity of attacks can range from mild to severe. They may occur daily, weekly, monthly, or not happen for years at a time. One thing is certain: Panic takes a heavy toll on a child's development because it affects every facet of his or her life.

Why Does My Child Have Panic Disorder?

No one knows for sure how or why a panic disorder develops, but it is believed to be triggered by a complex combination of factors that include biological and psychological influences, major life changes or trauma, medical conditions, or other mental disorders.

Biology/Heredity/Psychological Theories

Biological theories include that imbalances in the brain's neurotransmitters create a hyperreaction to environmental elements like light, noise, and movement or that the brain's amygdala, which controls fear, somehow is out of sync.

Genetics and heredity are thought to play a role in panic disorders. Children whose parents or relatives are chronically anxious are at a higher risk. Psychological theories target distorted thinking and reaction to bodily sensations, coping skills, and how feelings and emotions are expressed.

Parenting, Family, and Life Changes

Family patterns play a part in the development of a panic disorder. Parental attitudes and beliefs about the world influence a child's reaction to it. When parents are anxious and nervous about life, their children learn to be fearful, too. Children whose parents are perfectionists, overprotective, unresponsive, or abusive are more likely to develop anxiety disorders. Major life changes and trauma such as divorce or death of a parent, chronic illness, or abuse can trigger panic, as well as moving to a new school or adjusting to a new baby in the house.

Medical Conditions, Mental Disorders, and Learning Disabilities

Medical conditions such as allergies, asthma or other pulmonary diseases, thyroid problems, hypoglycemia, mitral valve prolapse (a benign heart condition), chronic hyperventilation, and Ménière's syndrome can create symptoms common to panic, which can lead to an actual attack. Children with learning disabilities or attention-deficit hyperactivity disorder (ADHD) are at a higher risk for school anxiety because of their chronic worry about trying to keep up in class and their feelings of helplessness and hopelessness. Students with physical disabilities may struggle with schoolwork or feel separate and lonely because classmates often avoid them. Mental conditions such as depression and other anxiety disorders increase the risk of developing a panic disorder.

Medications and Drug Use

Over-the-counter and prescription medications for asthma, thyroid conditions, colds, and allergies can all cause panic-like symptoms. Other substances to monitor include stimulants, such as caffeine found in soft drinks, which can cause hyperactivity, shaking, trembling, and dizziness and steroids used to enhance sports performance. Although recreational drug use generally begins between seventh and twelfth grade, children from fourth grade on are known to use inhalants, found in hundreds of common household products such as glue, shoe polish, felt tip markers, and gasoline. Inhalants create a high that leads to anxiety symptoms such as rapid heartbeat, dizziness, and feelings of being out of control, and some inhalants can cause death.

How Do Panic Disorder and Agoraphobia Impact My Child's School Experience?

For a child with a panic disorder, the school environment can seem impossible to manage because an attack can occur at any moment and there is no freedom to flee to immediate safety. The common worries of panic-stricken students include the following:

- Persistent worry about having an attack with no escape and being embarrassed in front of teachers and classmates
- Difficulty separating from home and adjusting to school
- Fear of participating in class; feeling isolated from others
- Problems concentrating in class while taking tests or doing homework
- Feelings of low self-worth in academic or social settings

Children with a panic disorder also feel ashamed and insecure. The long-term negative effects of panic include living in a shrinking, rigid world to avoid the possibility of an attack; being unable to learn and reach one's potential; being at risk of dropping out of high school or college; poor job prospects; broken personal relationships; or alcohol and drug abuse.

What Treatment Is Available for My Child?

Watching your child struggle with panic attacks is painful. You may feel helpless and hopeless about being able to calm your child's angst. However, panic can be alleviated with numerous methods and treatments. Your child can overcome it and flourish in school and in life.

Traditional Treatments

Cognitive-behavioral therapy (CBT) is a short-term method of treatment that emphasizes changing thinking patterns and reactions to anxiety-producing stimuli. Psychodynamic psychotherapists concentrate on emotions and introspection. Family therapy looks at family dynamics and helps with communication and making positive changes at home.

Antidepressants including selective serotonin reuptake inhibitors (SSRIs), such as Paxil, are commonly prescribed to treat panic disorder symptoms. Tricyclics and monoamine oxidase inhibitors (MAOIs) are also used, but less frequently for children. Benzodiazepines (antianxiety medications), such as Ativan, are often given in conjunction with SSRIs for faster symptom relief. A more detailed discussion about medication and conventional treatments is found in Chapter 19.

Nontraditional Treatments

Nontraditional treatments for panic disorders include diaphragmatic breathing, systematic desensitization, yoga, martial arts, regular physical exercise, diet, and teamwork with school personnel. Small changes in household routines, like reducing stress on school mornings (see Chapter 2 for suggestions on how to ease the morning rush) and making time for family fun, can be beneficial.

Overcoming Panic Attack Clinic

Watching your child live in fear is heartbreaking and frustrating. If agoraphobia is present, you watch your child's world becoming smaller by the minute as he tries to avoid any place or situation where an attack might occur. Attempting to reason with him that nothing bad will happen even though he is frightened is like trying to stop a runaway train: Seemingly you can't. That is, unless you know which switch to pull. The following guidelines and exercises will teach you how to help your child overcome panic. It will take determination, practice, and time. Your child can do it!

✎ Guidelines for Helping Your Child Overcome Panic

1. Never yell at, punish, or demean your child because of anxiety or allow family members, friends, or others to do so.
2. Teach your child, yourself, and your family how to relax. Learn self-help techniques for conquering panic and agoraphobia. If you had or have panic, do not discuss it at length with your child; she needs you to be strong for her.
3. Educate yourself and your child about the physical and emotional aspects of panic attacks. If your child's panic is severe, get professional help quickly.
4. Remain calm when your child has a panic attack. Comfort him and let him express how he feels. Tell him the feelings are a "false alarm." He survived the symptoms before and they will pass soon.
5. Applaud every small step your child takes to overcome panic, because small steps can add up to big victories.
6. Gently but firmly insist that your child attend school, but plan strategies with him to cope when he has an attack and feels trapped.

Meet with your child's teacher, guidance counselor, and other school personnel to come up with a plan to help your child succeed in school. The plan may include interventions for making transitions less stressful, creating a desensitization program, being able to discreetly alert the teacher that an attack is occurring so your child can leave the classroom without a fuss to a predetermined safe place, allowing extra time or a safe place for tests and in-class assignments, and establishing when to intervene in social situations.

Systematic Desensitization

Systematic desensitization (SD) is an effective behavioral treatment for anxiety disorders. In this counterconditioning technique, an anxious child is taught to relax deeply, then in small steps to face the fear while relaxing instead of panicking. When the child can relax during one step, the next step is faced. In the first part of the exercise, the child uses imagined desensitization. In the second, the child uses reality desensitization.

The process begins with creating a hierarchy of fears. Big overwhelming fears, such as test anxiety, are broken down into small, manageable steps. Each step is rated on the School Anxiety Scale in Chapter 16. One fear is worked on at a time. SD is effective for specific fears, agoraphobia, and the free-floating anxiety common to panic attacks.

CREATING A SCHOOL ANXIETY HIERARCHY

1. Together with your child make a list of fears.
2. Rank fears from least to most disturbing, choosing the least fearful situation first.
3. With your child, decide on clear defined goals for the fear.
4. Break down the goals into as many tiny steps as possible. Between eight and ten steps per goal is advisable, because you want the steps to be small and easily achievable in relationship to your child's fear in order to build confidence.
5. If your child cannot relax at a step, either go back to the previous step or break the step into smaller pieces.
6. Rate each step on the School Anxiety Scale to get a starting point, and to chart progress.

✎ Example of a School Anxiety Hierarchy

Main Fear: Taking a test
Goals: I want to take the test feeling confident, and get a grade of B or above.

1. Teacher says, "Next week is a test." Rating: 5
2. Thinking about the test that is one week away. Rating: 2
3. Reviewing test material in class. Rating: 3
4. Studying for the test. Rating: 6–7
5. Going to bed the night before the test. Rating: 7½
6. Waking up the morning of the test, thinking about it. Rating: 8
7. Getting ready for school the morning of the test. Rating: 7–8
8. Leaving for school the day of the test; riding the bus. Rating: 8½
9. Walking into school. Rating: 9
10. Waiting for the test to be handed out. Rating: 9½
11. Teacher handing out the test. Rating: 10
12. Looking at the test. Rating: 10
13. Taking the test. Rating: 9–10

Anxiety will usually plummet when the test is over, but could remain high if a child worries about having done poorly on it. Another anxious spike could come when the graded test is returned, and depending on the grade, could continue if parental consequences for a poor grade are an issue.

✎ Guidelines for Systematic Desensitization

1. Your child must be able to relax quickly and at will—review all chapters on relaxation.
2. She must be able to visualize the details of the feared situation.
3. Do not skip steps on the hierarchy even if the child feels better after the first few steps.
4. Read about "feared scenes" in Chapter 16, "Learning to Let Go and Flow."
5. Expect setbacks. Anxiety symptoms decrease and increase during the SD process, and can even spike again on a com-

pleted step. If that occurs, just work on that step again until the child feels comfortable; then move on.

6. Do not make a rigid timetable to reach goals as that is a setup for failure.
7. Praise your child's effort, not only the end result.
8. Rate each completed step on the School Anxiety Scale with your child to reinforce the progress made.
9. This is hard work, especially for a child. Be patient!

The ideal way to ease anxiety with SD is to practice with imagined desensitization first, then move on to the reality desensitization. However, with school fears, your child has no control in deciding when he is ready to really take a test or be called on in class to answer a question. To remedy that, practice each step one at a time. Decrease the number of steps in the hierarchy, and have your child imagine each step from beginning to end while being relaxed. Repeat daily, if necessary.

DESENSITIZING YOUR CHILD

1. Have your child either lie down or sit in a comfortable chair.
2. Tell him to imagine the first step on his hierarchy, and then rate it on the School Anxiety Scale.
3. Tell him to keep imagining the step, begin belly breathing, and use other relaxation techniques until anxious feelings subside. Ask him to rate his anxiety now on the scale.
4. Depending on his level of anxiety and difficulty facing the real situation, either do another step or stop.
5. Practice every day. When your child can relax quickly while imagining the step, move to the next one.

When the steps are finished, make plans with him to begin facing the fear in reality. As the next step in the desensitization process, you might role-play fearful situations with your child. For example, at home have him practice test taking, dealing with a bully, or being called on in class. If the thought of trying the real thing scares him, make the steps smaller by having him practice in fantasy and role-play again until he is ready for the real thing.

Some children are too young or too anxious to engage in systematic desensitization; if so, don't force it. Continue teaching a variety of relaxation exercises, be physically active, decrease your own stress and that of your family, cut down on foods that negatively affect blood sugar levels, build your child's confidence, and make time for family fun. With patience, determination, practice, teamwork with the school, and clinical help if necessary, your child can successfully conquer school anxiety.

CHAPTER 6

My Child Fears People, Places, and Things

CHILDREN WITH PHOBIAS OR IRRATIONAL FEARS CAN HAVE A hard time going to school. Then they have to remain at school all day long, where avoiding the source of their fear may not be possible or trying to do so might cause embarrassment.

Second grader Abby has been afraid of spiders since first grade, after a large spider crawled over her head and face. One day in class, she saw a spider on the floor and was so afraid it would crawl on her that she panicked and froze until it was out of sight. Abby spent the rest of the day looking around for the spider and couldn't concentrate on class work. Her teacher noticed how distracted she was, but Abby felt ashamed to say what was wrong. Now every day in school is tense, as she waits for the spider to appear.

Jack, a fifth grader, is uncomfortable in social settings, or ones where he has to perform, such as being called on in class, because he feels inadequate in comparison to other children. If he is made to be the center of attention, he can't turn off his thoughts that people are laughing at him and thinking he is stupid.

Abby's fear is a specific phobia, Jack struggles with social phobia, and both children are suffering. This chapter covers different types of phobias, their causes, the various methods of treatment to conquer phobias, and guidelines and exercises to help your child overcome his or her fears.

What Are Phobias?

Childhood fears and behaviors such as your eight-month-old's fear of strangers, your toddler's fear of being flushed down the toilet, or your five-year-old's screaming and clinging to your leg on the first day of school are normal developmental fears and reactions. Remember, young children up to about the age of six are literal in their thinking and may confuse their imaginary thoughts with reality. Other normal childhood fears are the dark, monsters, sleeping alone, and staying with a babysitter. As a child matures and adjusts to the larger world, these fears pass.

Phobic fear is different. *Phobia* comes from the Greek word meaning "fear." Phobias are the most common anxiety disorder; the National Institute of Mental Health (NIMH) estimates that between 5 percent and up to 21 percent of all Americans develop a phobia at some point in their lives.

Unlike the normal fear that children and adults feel at times, phobic fear is the excessive, irrational fear of people, places, things, and situations, causing a change in behavior, and is one of the anxiety disorders. A phobic reaction occurs due to a specific trigger such as seeing a spider, being afraid of water, having blood drawn, or socializing. The fear reaction can be mild, with few symptoms, or severe, with all of the symptoms of a heart-pounding panic attack that could lead to avoidance of the feared object.

Many phobias are directed at benign objects, such as the fear of rabbits (leporiphobia); some fears are of dangerous things, such as wild animals (agrizoophobia) and tornados (lilapsophobia), or of things that cause pain, such as injections (trypanophobia); others are rare or seem strange, such as the fear of looking up (anablephobia). Any way a child's fear manifests, the majority of children outgrow phobias. Those who don't will likely take chronic phobias into adulthood and run a high risk of developing other anxiety disorders, such as panic disorder.

Does My Child Have a Phobia?

When your child encounters a thing, person, or circumstance that provokes a nervous reaction, do any of the following physical symptoms occur?

- Shallow, rapid breathing; racing heart; palpitations; or chest pain
- Sweating and flushing
- Stomachache, diarrhea, nausea, or vomiting
- Headaches, dizziness, or shakiness

Young children and even older ones often do not realize that their distress is unreasonable in the situation. They take their fears literally, so trying to rationalize with a phobic child can be impossible. If questioned about what is bothering them, many children can't state exactly why they are so frightened or don't believe that they are not in danger.

Taylor, in first grade, is afraid of dogs, cats, squirrels, birds, or anything with fur or feathers that he feels might attack him or climb on him. School is hard for Taylor because even looking at pictures of animals or seeing animal puppets sets his heart racing and makes him want to flee. Schoolbooks with animal pictures, games, and art projects all have the potential of triggering Taylor's phobic reaction. When a classmate brought in her rabbit to show the class, he had to go to the nurse's office. Since then, he regularly throws tantrums on school mornings wanting to stay home. Taylor cannot be reasoned with or reassured that the pet rabbit or picture of one can't hurt him.

Children commonly express their fears through behavior rather than verbal explanation. The following behaviors are exhibited by children when faced with a phobic trigger:

- Crying and clinging
- Freezing (not being able to move)

- Angry outbursts, yelling, screaming, or tantrums
- Electing not to speak, eat, or write around certain people or in certain situations
- Avoiding phobic triggers: people, places, things, social or performance situations

A phobic reaction can be triggered by pictures, photos, or images on TV, on the computer, or in movies of the feared object as well as things or situations that resemble it.

Mary, a kindergartner, is afraid of riding in cars since she was in a fender bender. Her fear has spread to other modes of transportation such as the school bus, planes, and trains. Even watching a movie that shows a car, bus, plane, or train or seeing pictures of these things jump-starts her anxiety.

When fears are not due to normal developmental stages or persist for more than a few weeks, your child will need to be evaluated by your family physician and a mental health specialist.

What Are Specific Phobias?

A specific phobia is the illogical fear of being harmed or losing control when exposed to a clearly defined object or situation, for example, being afraid of dogs who could bite or not wanting to fly because the plane might crash. While some dogs do bite and some planes crash, the majority do not—phobic fear is out of proportion to the actual danger of the situation or circumstance. Other examples are being afraid of a dog who is friendly and leashed or panicking on a plane during a noneventful flight.

Specific phobias are divided into the following five categories:

1. *Animal Type.* This phobia includes animals and insects, for example, cats (ailurphobia) and spiders (arachnophobia).
2. *Natural Environment Type.* This phobia includes thunder

and lightning (astraphobia), heights (acrophobia), and water (hydrophobia).

3. *Blood-Injection/Injury Type.* This phobia may include getting an injection (trypanophobia), seeing a classmate scrape a knee and bleed (hemaphobia), or visiting the school nurse/doctor (iatrophobia).

4. *Situational Type.* These phobias occur in situations like going over bridges (gephyrophobia), using public transportation, or being in other enclosed places (claustrophobia).

5. *Other Type.* This last category includes behaviors such as the fear of choking (pnigophobia), vomiting (emetophobia), or having a disease (nosophobia). Lists of hundreds of phobias can be found on the Internet.

Children with a specific phobia do not display the widespread anxiety associated with panic disorder because their fear is set off by a specific object or situation, not the "fear of the fear." But a generalized anticipatory anxiety could develop if the child has to encounter the feared thing on a regular basis, for example, being afraid of using a computer (technophobia) and having to use one every day in school. Depending on the phobia and severity of the child's reaction, phobic children may think and worry about their phobias a good part of the day, or expend energy trying to avoid them. When that occurs, it will be very hard to concentrate in class, develop friendships, or have fun.

Jaden, a third grader, became terrified of storms and lightning after a sudden electrical storm hit while he was waiting for his mother to pick him up after school. She was a few minutes late that day, and he was terrified that she had forgotten him and that the lightning would kill him. Sensitive and considered a "worrier" by his parents, Jaden now checks the weather every school morning. Even overcast days are enough to get him anxious and asking to stay home. His grades are falling because he is unable to focus in the classroom due to his obsession with looking out the window hundreds of times a day to see if clouds are forming. Although Jaden is social with lots of friends, his phobia is spreading to fears about going to friends' houses to play if the weather is cloudy or if the potential for rain or a storm exists, so he stays home most of the time.

What Is Social Phobia?

Social phobia, also called social anxiety, is a pronounced, unrelenting fear of being embarrassed and humiliated in daily social situations. Social phobia is not shyness. It is more severe, and according to NIMH, about 1 percent of children in the United States will develop the disorder.

Children with social anxiety often have fears around activities in school and do not recognize that their fears are generally baseless, for example, the fear of talking to classmates because of being labeled stupid; the fear of being called on by the teacher; the fear of performing in front of others; and the fear of test taking, meeting strangers, or reading aloud in class. The fear develops without any evidence that the children are a target and will be laughed at and humiliated. A feared situation will bring on acute anxiety, which could become an all-out panic attack and lead to severe distress and avoidance.

Cheryl is developing a social phobia that is negatively affecting her in school. She is in fourth grade, tall and lanky, and although not the tallest in her class feels that she towers over everyone, that she is on display, and that other students are staring at her or talking about her. She worries about being stared at all day long at school but doesn't see her reaction as being over the top. Although naturally shy, she was well liked by her peers, but this year she has begun to shun extracurricular school activities and interacting with friends and classmates. Friends are beginning to stop trying to socialize with her or invite her to spend time with them, and she thinks she has heard some classmates call her "weird." The thought of trying to make new friends terrifies her. Cheryl feels isolated at school and although she goes without complaint, she feels great distress and has physical symptoms, such as stomachaches and diarrhea. She can hardly concentrate in class and her grades are falling.

Children with social phobia experience the same heart-pounding symptoms as those with panic disorder, but the worries about being embarrassed and triggers that jump-start the fears are specific to performance anxiety, and include those in the following list:

- Fears of being teased, criticized, or judged by others, especially when the center of attention
- Extreme self-consciousness and anxiety in everyday social situations, such as eating in the school lunchroom; feeling "on stage," "not liked," or that people are staring at them.
- Feeling panicky when meeting new people, having to speak in public, or attend social events

The main school fears are test taking, being called on in class, going to the board, giving a speech, performing in any way in front of others, or having to interact with classmates and school personnel. Children may show their distress in any of the following ways:

- Complaining of stomachaches; headaches; feeling dizzy, clammy, or sweaty; and blushing
- Avoiding eye contact
- Being jittery, fidgety, shaky, or trembly
- Speaking inaudibly or in a whisper
- Refusing to go to school

In rare cases, some children refuse to speak at all in certain situations, for example, in school or at the doctor's office, but can speak and choose to do so where they feel safe. This rare type of social phobia is called selective mutism. Agoraphobia may develop if the fear of being trapped in places or situations where escape might be difficult or embarrassing becomes overwhelming. Read Chapter 5, "My Child Panics and Avoids Situations," for additional information on panic attacks and agoraphobia.

Whatever the subject of the fear—people, places, things, or situations—children who have phobias are consumed by their worry, experience high anxiety, and exhibit avoidance behavior.

Why Is My Child Phobic?

Phobias are complex disorders and develop due to a combination of factors. The causes of phobias include having a negative face-to-face or a traumatic experience with the feared person, thing, or situation; witnessing a bad experience; watching parents or other influential people react with fear to certain people, things, or situations; or hearing frightening stories about these things.

Psychological theories include repressed, displaced, or unresolved emotions; distorted thinking; or hypersensitivity to bodily sensations and external situations. Physiological causes examine abnormalities in the brain's neurotransmitters or areas linked to exaggerated emotional responses to certain stimuli. Genetics seems to play a role, with many phobic children having at least one parent with an anxiety disorder.

Children who have learning disorders or have diseases or conditions that result in physical malformation, such as cerebral palsy, have a hard time "fitting in" and should be monitored for social anxiety. Shyness and behavioral inhibition (the tendency for babies to be cautious or withdrawn with new people or situations) seem to be precursors to the development of social phobia and are inherited. Children with these tendencies and those who exhibit anxiety need encouragement and guidance to handle the stress of school and social interactions.

What Treatment Is Available for My Child?

Phobias are traditionally treated using a combination of exposure therapy and systematic desensitization, which allows children to face their fears one step at a time while remaining relaxed and calm. Cognitive therapy helps children understand their negative thoughts and then challenges them to think about things differently. Psychodynamic therapies allow children to emotionally work through serious issues that may have caused the initial phobic reaction. Therapy for children is a mixture of talk and play. Medication is less often prescribed for a specific phobia than for social phobia, because exposure and behavioral therapies have a high rate of success for specific phobia.

Alternative treatments shown to help children overcome phobias include relaxation techniques, massage, yoga, hypnotherapy, and acupressure. For a detailed description of traditional and alternative therapies, see Chapters 19 and 20.

Overcoming Phobia Clinic

Trying to reassure your child that he is not in danger when he is faced with a phobic situation is a tough sell. Nevertheless, giving him the tools to face his fears will empower him and put him on the path to recovery. The following guidelines and exercises will help you to do that.

✎ Guidelines for Helping Your Child Overcome Phobias

1. Do not tease, ridicule, or punish your child because of his fears or allow others to do so. His fears are real to him.
2. Allow your child to tell you how he feels. Listen without judgment.
3. If you have phobias, get help immediately so you can be a good role model. Do not discuss your phobias with your child. Be there for him.
4. Support your child, but do not enable his behavior. For example, do not react with tension or deliberately avoid the situation, like crossing the street if he sees a cat. Instead, remain calm and encourage him to face the fear and stay in the situation.
5. Teach him relaxation, stress management, and coping strategies. Use them yourself and teach everyone in the family to use them.
6. Encourage him to invite friends over to play, to visit friends, to go to parties, and to have sleepovers. Don't force it, but help him to slowly go out into the world.
7. Encourage participation in clubs, sports, and organizations

where he can build his confidence and make friends around a shared interest.

Do not try to rush his progress, because tackling anxiety takes patience, practice, and time. Don't set him up to fail. Follow his pace and problem solve with him. Teach him that small victories add up to big ones.

Exercises

The following exercises can be used for either specific or social phobia. Groups of exercises that are prerequisites are False Alarm Explanation (Chapter 2); Systematic Desensitization and Creating Hierarchy of Fears (Chapter 5); Breathing (Chapter 14); Staying in the Moment (Chapter 15); and Let Go and Flow (Chapter 16). Art supplies used are a large drawing pad, colored pencils, crayons, paint, brushes, Silly Putty or clay, Legos or blocks, dollhouses and toy figures, newspapers, magazines, photos of your child that can be cut out or pasted, scissors, glue, and tape.

DEMYSTIFYING THE FEAR THROUGH CREATIVE EXPRESSION

With your child create a hierarchy of fears ranking them from least fearful to most. Explain to your child that he is going to face his fears by creating them out of art materials of his choice such as collage materials, drawing materials, or clay, or by using dollhouses and toys. As he works, if his anxiety surfaces, have him stop, breathe, and use any of the anxiety-reducing techniques that he has learned. Also, ask your child how he would handle the real situation. When he finishes a project, ask him how he feels about the fear now, and rank it on the anxiety scale. Save what he created for practice, and have him look at it daily while he relaxes until it loses its power over him.

- *Making a Collage.* Cut out pictures of his fears such as animals, insects, storms, water, children in school, playing with friends, and so on, and create a collage. Have him paste a photo of himself somewhere in the midst of his fears.

- *Sculpting the Phobia.* Using clay or Silly Putty, have your child build a phobic thing or scene. Suggest he put himself in his creation as a way to face his fear. Save it for practice.
- *Drawing/Painting the Phobia.* Have the child draw or paint his fears and try to get him to put himself in the picture.
- *Building the Phobia.* Create the phobia out of blocks or other building materials and toys, putting himself in the scene.

When your child feels secure so that he can relax while in the feared situation, plan with him how he is going to practice in the real world. For example, go to a pet store to look at dogs, and then pet a puppy; look out the window at an electrical storm; call a friend to play or accept a birthday party invitation; raise his hand in class; or join a school club.

Variation on Demystifying Phobias

Take your child to the library or bookstore and find books about the specific phobia he has, for example. learn about spiders, electrical storms, dogs, wild animals, blood, or oceans. Find educational movies or TV shows to watch with him. For social phobia, find stories and movies about children who had his problem and overcame it. Have your child write his own story or do it in drawings, poetry, or song.

Role-Playing

Explain to your child that you and she are going to rehearse her new skills in coping with situations that make her uncomfortable. And that the more she practices, the more confident she will become when she faces the real situation. First, decide on which feared situation she wants to start with. Ask her if she would like to write a script to follow or talk about what she will be doing. Then set up a simulation of the scene at home by creating a home classroom to practice raising her hand or going to the board. Make believe she is calling a friend on the phone to set up a play date. Pretend she is walking into a friend's birthday party. Decide with your child which relaxation techniques she will use, and what your role is, for example, teacher or friend. Begin role-playing, having your child practice relaxation techniques through-out the scene. With practice, she'll build confidence in real situations. Practice should be timed to your child's age and attention span. Stop role-playing if she wants to or if you observe that she is struggling and cannot relax quickly.

Phobias are powerful fears and overcoming them will likely take many weeks or months. Be patient. Remember that progress is one step for-ward, and two back. It is the discipline of practice that will build your child's confidence to face her fears one exercise at a time.

CHAPTER 7

My Child Has Homework Anxiety

ᕙᕗ

MOST STUDENTS DISLIKE DOING HOMEWORK, BUT DO IT BE-grudgingly. Children who feel anxious about going to school or test taking may also exhibit apprehension when faced with homework.

Eva, a fifth grader who was diagnosed with the learning disability dyslexia, spends hours filled with anxiety and cries over homework assignments. Third grader Josh, who does not have a learning disability, also finds it tough to finish his homework, refusing to do it most days, and argues frequently with his parents about it.

Since homework has become a standard often starting in kindergarten, it is crucial to help your anxious child conquer homework fears, so he can not only thrive academically and socially but also be excited about wanting to learn.

Homework Starts in Kindergarten

When you sent your child off to kindergarten, she may have returned with something unexpected—homework. Yet, from kindergarten on your child will almost certainly be facing homework assignments. Many educators and parents are proponents for homework in the early grades. They claim that homework is important for a number of reasons: It reinforces the work covered in class that day; prepares students for the next day; and teaches good study habits, time management, and how to work independently. It also acts as a bridge between parent and school, keeps parents up-to-date on what their child is learning, and tries to foster a love of learning in the student. As a parent of a child with homework anxiety, you know that the ideal benefits from homework are not always the reality of the situation.

There is a recent groundswell of parents and educators who oppose giving homework in the early years. They believe that today's student is overloaded with too much homework, which creates stress and anxiety in both child and family. Overloading children with homework leaves them little time for play and creative activities, relaxing family time, and other important after-school activities necessary for positive childhood development. In some school districts, parents have organized and been instrumental in changing school policy regarding homework. See the resources section at the end of this book for more information if you are interested in reducing the homework load for your child.

How Much Homework Is Right for My Child?

Each child is different in how his or her academic ability develops, but a rule of thumb suggested by many educational organizations is that children from kindergarten through first grade get ten minutes of homework each day, and second to third grade get twenty minutes, with ten minutes added as the student moves up in grade. Reading or other projects may be separate from homework assignments and will add to the time. Parental involvement is necessary, especially in the lower grades, to help with time management, to make sure assignments are completed, and to offer necessary help.

Many children have little problem completing a fair amount of homework. But for others it's not a ten- to twenty-minute learning experience, but a daily nightmare that can drag on for hours, take up time on the weekend, test parents' patience, and leave children feeling devastated about their abilities and down on school and learning.

Christy is in first grade. She is nervous about separating from home on school mornings and begs to stay home or says she has a stomachache. School anxiety makes it hard for her to concentrate on lessons in class. Every day Christy brings home a worksheet or activity that must be completed with her parents' help, such as writing a sentence about a book she read, in addition to reading for twenty minutes a day. When her mother tells her it is time to do homework, Christy starts to cry because it reminds her that she'll have to go back to school. It can take a tense hour or more for Christy to get the work completed, leaving both she and her mother exhausted.

Kareem is in third grade. He just can't sit still for long periods of time, so being in school all day is tough for him. Kareem jiggles in his seat, can't stay focused for more than a few minutes, and sometimes gets up and disrupts his class. Faced with daily homework assignments such as completing skill sheets, studying spelling words, reading a science study guide and notes, and completing math problems, Kareem often does not bring home his assignments; he stuffs them in the back of his desk. When he is faced with having to do homework, instead of thirty minutes of learning, Kareem's parents have to endure hours of his tantrums and screaming trying to get him to sit down. Kareem has begun to say he hates school and won't go.

Michelle, in sixth grade, is a nervous, tense girl who is a perfectionist. She always did her homework, got good grades, and was also active in sports and other activities. This year, however, the homework load is getting to be too much for her. She feels overwhelmed by daily assignments that could include completing spelling worksheets; doing a creative-writing exercise; completing multiple math worksheets; and reading and writing in geography, science, and Spanish. When she sits down to begin homework and looks at the pile of books, she groans about the hours of work ahead of her. Lately, Michelle has been feeling panicky and her sense of dread around homework makes it difficult for her to concentrate and work effectively. She's feeling down a good deal of the time and is thinking of giving up all outside activities.

All of these students need some kind of intervention: Christy to work through separation anxiety and to adjust to school and homework structure; Kareem to be evaluated for learning and attention problems, and to learn how to concentrate and focus; and Michelle to learn how to take that big pile of work and make it manageable. Children who suffer from homework anxiety may act out their apprehension in the following ways:

- Become increasingly stressed when faced with homework
- Forget to bring assignments home, or usually deny having any work assigned
- Try to get out of going to school
- Exhibit anxiety symptoms, such as frequent stomachaches, headaches, shortness of breath, or tightness in the chest when faced with doing homework or projects
- Have trouble sleeping
- Have tantrums or often be angry and irritable when doing homework
- Show symptoms of depression or be sad and withdrawn

When homework anxiety is serious, it causes daily emotional pain and suffering, lowers self-confidence, is isolating, and blocks emotional well-being and academic growth. Finding out why homework anxiety is present will help you to take the necessary steps to begin to help your child.

The Causes of Homework Anxiety

Children who suffer from anxiety or have been diagnosed with an anxiety disorder, such as panic disorder, are more apt to be easily overwhelmed by class work and its partner homework. These children often find it difficult to concentrate on subject content, think through home-work assignments, and organize the material and their time because much of their energy is spent trying to cope with their uncomfortable anxiety symptoms.

Children with learning and attention problems struggle with home-work. Students with learning problems face the daily frustration of trying to keep up with class work. They worry about failing and being embarrassed in front of their class. For these children, having to face homework every day creates added stress, and their struggle with it can reinforce their feelings about being different from the rest of the class, and believing they are stupid and losers.

Family conflict or major life changes, such as divorce or moving to a new school, can make it difficult for children to be able to concentrate in school and on homework. A child whose life is in flux is at a high risk of developing anxiety or of becoming depressed, causing stress to be high and coping skills to be low. Homework anxiety can also occur if children do not have a quiet safe place to work, or no adults are available to provide structure and guidance to help children form good study habits.

Not "fitting in," being teased or bullied, or having to deal with a troubling relationship with a teacher or other school staff may be creating anxiety around anything to do with school, including homework.

Some children get too much homework for their grade. They are overloaded with assignments, worksheets, and projects that are just too much for them to handle. No matter how much they try, they never finish, or do so with extreme difficulty, setting them up for failure. If you believe this is the problem, then take your case to the school and district.

Children may not want to talk about what is troubling them, but gentle questioning and support for your child's feelings should help him to talk to you about what is troubling him. Contact your school immediately to schedule an appointment with teachers and other school personnel to get to the bottom of the problem. If you suspect that your child has an anxiety disorder, contact your family physician and get a referral to a mental health specialist.

Overcoming Homework Anxiety Clinic

Your reactions to your child's homework anxiety will play an important role in her overcoming it. There are important skills and techniques that aid in managing and taming the homework beast that any child can learn. Read on and set your child up for success.

✎ Guidelines for Helping Your Child with Homework Anxiety

1. Talk to your child about her fears, find out what is troubling her, and reassure her that you support her and that together you will find solutions to her problem. Do not make fun of or demean your child about her fears, or let anyone else do so.

2. Communicate frequently with your child's teacher. Keep up-to-date with what work is required, and with what is happening in the classroom. Ask the teacher what rules and guidelines to follow regarding homework, such as how closely to monitor your child's work. Spend time in your child's classroom to find out what and how the work is taught.

3. Control your frustration and anger if your child does not want to do homework. Be firm but kind about her having to complete homework assignments, and tell her that you will be available to help and support her efforts. Tell your child that homework is part of her job and be clear about expectations.

4. Decide with your child where her homework workspace will be. Make it comfortable and special. For example, help your child paint or decorate her own homework space or desk. Remember, some children like to change their homework venue; sometimes they may work on the kitchen table, other times their bedroom. Be flexible with their decision.

5. Create a flexible homework schedule with your child, how much time she needs to spend, and when and where it will

be done. When it is completed, reward your child with appropriate praise, time spent with you, a special TV show, and so on.

6. Check your child's homework when it is finished, and review any teacher comments on returned assignments with your child.

7. Limit TV and computer time. Find educational programs, reading material, creative projects, and activities that reinforce the content of the homework.

8. Make reading and learning an important family pursuit that is fun and exciting.

Other to-dos include not expecting perfection from your child; perfection will set him up to fail. Instead, teach him by example how to accept making mistakes, constructive criticism, and even failure, and then how to learn from these things. De-stress your life as much as possible, practice the relaxation exercises, and teach them to your child and other family members.

Exercises: What You Need to Do and Have on Hand

Read through the exercises before you begin. Prerequisites for these exercises include being able to relax quickly: know breathing (Chapter 14), learn staying in the moment (Chapter 15), and be able to let go and float (Chapter 16). With your child, choose a place to do homework that is comfortable and free from distractions. Decide on what rewards your child will have during the five-minute homework breaks. Ideas are to have a healthy snack, free time, a story or part of one, putting the pieces of a puzzle together, and so on—but breaks do not exceed five minutes. Determine how long your child will work, making it age appropriate. Start with a short time, five minutes on and five off, or ten on and five off, and gradually lengthen work time as the child's anxiety eases and confidence and abilities increase. If your child holds or touches something to stay in the moment—for example, some children like to touch a favorite toy or stuffed animal, or a smooth stone that they can rub between their fingers—have that on the work table. You will also need an alarm clock.

MANAGING THE HOMEWORK LOAD

Tell your child that you are going to help her feel less stressed about homework by breaking up the pile of work into small pieces that she can handle. She will do homework for a predetermined amount of time and then she will get to take a five-minute rest and choose one reward, then work, rest, and so on until homework is completed. The completed work will be put away (it does not exist anymore), and the next assignment taken out (for right now, this is the only homework she has). This is repeated until all homework is finished.

BREATHING THROUGH HOMEWORK

1. Have your child place all of the homework on the table.
2. Ask her what assignment she wants to work on first. Put it aside.
3. Tell your child that she is going to do a "staying-in-the-moment" exercise. Now have her take all of the other books and papers and put them away in a closet or another room. Say to her, "See, they don't exist anymore. You're only going to concentrate on the moment, doing the work in front of you."
4. Have her belly breathe for two to three minutes.
5. Set the clock for the desired work time. Have her work until the alarm goes off, and then take a five-minute break. Belly breathe throughout this exercise. Repeat until all homework is finished.
6. If anxiety crops up before work time is up, have her stop immediately, breathe, relax, then start again.
7. Use Breathing Through Homework as a daily structure until your child can work independently and without anxiety.

If your child stops working because she does not understand something, urge her to not stop but to try to work it out on her own, and continue belly breathing. Remember anxious children get upset easily and have a tendency to give up when they are challenged. If after a few minutes she can't do the work, help her.

TROUBLESHOOTING

If your child is young, or has severe homework anxiety and doesn't believe that breaking homework into small pieces will make it less stressful, try this: Show your child an apple and say, "I want you to try to eat this apple without taking bites from it or cutting it up into pieces." Of course it won't fit into her mouth. Then have her take bites or cut up the apple. "See, now it is easy to eat. It's the same with homework. We're going to take small bites out of it so it goes down easier."

For a child who has panicked during homework, just the thought of sitting down to do it may start the fight-or-flight response. To stop these symptoms, have her belly breathe and do any of the following exercises prior to starting homework: Use the finger touch exercise (Chapter 4), hold or touch a favorite item that she has practiced with during staying-in-the-moment exercises, focus on sitting in the chair, or place her arms flat on the table and concentrate on how that feels. As she does homework, whenever anxiety symptoms surface, have her stop, breathe, and use any of these techniques until the anxiety eases. Repeat as necessary. With practice and time, anxiety will become hardly a whisper.

When the homework load is causing very high anxiety, have your child stop working and have her either sit, stand, or lie down and use the letting go and floating technique in Chapter 16 until she rides out the wave of fear. As soon as the anxiety lessens, have her go back to her table and begin to work. Repeat as necessary. For severely homework-phobic students, a systematic desensitization program may have to be created. (See Chapter 5, "My Child Panics and Avoids Situations," for instructions.)

Another technique for reducing severe anxiety symptoms, and to build confidence, is to use the Imagining Worry exercise, explained at the end of Chapter 4. Tell your child that this is called Imagining

Homework. Have her picture herself doing homework, feeling the anxiety around it, and then relaxing into her anxious feelings using the relaxation techniques in this book. As the anxiety lessens, have her change her mental picture into seeing herself doing the homework in a calm state while feeling capable of doing it well and figuring out the work if she doesn't understand it. This exercise is best practiced at nonhomework times in bed or in a comfortable chair. Repeat at least three times a week.

No matter what a child's age, how long he has been anxious, or how severe the anxiety is, the guidelines, exercises, and techniques in this chapter will make a positive difference in stopping homework anxiety, as well as teaching good study habits and coping skills. The caveat is that it will take effort, determination, patience, practice, and time on the part of both parent and child. Although progress may be slow, don't give up; eventually it will work to your child's benefit.

CHAPTER 8

My Child Has Test Anxiety

෨

TEST ANXIETY IS ONE OF THE MOST COMMON CAUSES OF SCHOOL anxiety. Every student understands that taking a test means she will be graded, judged, and compared to her classmates, and that performing badly will likely net her negative consequences from her teacher and parents.

Michael, a first grader, has struggled with arithmetic since he began school, and is barely passing. Every time a math test is scheduled, he tries to avoid studying for it and cries and begs to stay home from school on test day.

Priscilla, a sixth grader, gets good grades but suffers in silence before any test, even on subjects she is getting an A in, with symptoms of stomach pain, diarrhea, and vomiting.

Ray, in third grade, can't stop himself from trembling before a spelling test, and although he studies and knows the work at home, he often can't remember how to spell the words during the tests, and gets low grades.

Children who experience the kind of test anxiety that creates distress or low test scores are at a disadvantage when it comes to being successful in the classroom. This chapter defines test anxiety and explains its causes, symptoms, and short- and long-term effects on children. Easy-to-learn exercises and techniques to help children conquer test anxiety are provided, along with parental guidelines.

Kindergarten Is Not Playtime Anymore

Over the last twenty-five years, there has been a shift in kindergarten curriculum from what is commonly called child-centered, or play-based programs, to skill-based or academic courses of study centering on reading and math. Along with this shift came a proliferation of testing from kindergarten to twelfth grade, with an increase in student stress and higher numbers of children who experience test anxiety. The No Child Left Behind Act of 2001 has made standardized testing even more important for students, teachers, and schools, because federal guidelines mandate that schools reach certain educational standards for every child within a specified time or be penalized.

Kindergarten once was an incubator to the transition to first grade, but today it is considered by many educators to be the "new first grade." Instead of story time, arts and crafts, sing-alongs, snacks, naps, and learning group dynamics, today's kindergartner may be spending a good deal of time doing worksheets to learn how to read and do math.

Testing may begin before a child enters kindergarten with such standardized tests as the Kindergarten Readiness Test (KRT). Students are assessed on their proficiency in vocabulary and their ability to identify letters, distinguish large and small differences between objects, recognize that language is made up of small sounds, comprehend what they have read and then interpret its meaning, and know numbers and understand math. Many children flourish within these new standards, but others feel like failures even before they walk through the classroom door.

Each state sets it academic standards, and school districts have leeway to do so too, so some schools have taken the academic approach, whereas others remain more child centered. If your child is struggling with testing, you need to find out your school's philosophy and take the necessary action to help your child.

What Is Test Anxiety?

"Good morning, class," the teacher said. "I have an announcement to make. This Friday, you're going to have a math test." Those words will make almost 100 percent of the students groan and a good percentage of them nervous. Being anxious about an upcoming test is normal and even necessary because students need a little adrenaline rush so they will be "up" for the test. Normal amounts of anxiety can add spark and vitality to the mental performance needed to test well. If your child gets anxious when a test is looming, but is able to study hard and for the most part tests well, then test anxiety is a nonissue. But if your child is distraught over testing, exhibits negative or acting-out behavioral changes, can't study, or tests poorly even when he has studied, then test anxiety is a problem.

Testing by its very nature is being judged and evaluated in relationship to one's peers. Students who test well generally feel smart and are more confident than poor testers. Students who dread tests often feel stupid and ashamed about their anxiety and poor grades and often suffer from low self-worth, not understanding that low test scores may not be an indication of true intelligence or ability. Test anxiety disturbs the mind and body in the way that any anxiety does, affecting children in how they think, learn, and reason; how they feel about school and themselves; and how they react to school and learning. Scoring low on tests may also cause negative responses from teachers and other students.

Denise, a ten-year-old fifth grader, can't sleep the night before a test, lying awake worrying that she will "blank out" during the test, won't remember a thing she studied, and will probably fail. Denise is right, because her brain freezes as soon as she looks at the first question. Sometimes she gives up, puts her name on the paper, and takes a zero. Denise is smart and understands the work, but her anxiety doesn't allow her to show that on tests.

Jamie, in second grade, can hardly sit still during a test. His heart pounds, his hands and legs shake, making him feel like he is going to jump out of his skin. When Jamie can't control his symptoms during a test, which is almost all the time, he feigns a stomachache and tries to be sent to the school nurse.

Shelly is in fourth grade. The first time she was tested in kindergarten, she looked at the paper and promptly vomited. Since then, taking tests is a nightmare for her. Shelly becomes irritable and has angry outbursts days before a test. Even thinking about the test makes her anxious, so she avoids studying. Shelly feels stupid and "different" from her classmates, and does not interact with them.

Katie always feels panicky before a test. She can't sleep the night before, feels nauseated and has diarrhea the morning of the test, and worries that she will fail. She feels an adrenaline rush when she gets the test paper, which scares her into thinking she will faint. However, she begins the test, and though she suffers, Katie usually tests well.

Denise, Jamie, and Shelly are all smart, but their test anxiety makes it almost impossible for them to show what they know and get good grades. Even their peer relationships are beginning to suffer because they all feel a sense of shame about their problems and shun many peer relationships. Katie's test scores are good, but her test anxiety creates high stress that she has trouble handling. Test anxiety in any form negatively affects the quality of a student's life.

Does My Child Have Test Anxiety?

Children with test anxiety can experience any number of physical, mental, and emotional symptoms, which can vary from mild to severe. Some children act out their anxiety in overt ways, whereas others suffer in silence. Physical symptoms include:

- Heart palpitations, shortness of breath, chest tightening/ pain, or sore throat

- Stomachache, nausea, vomiting, or diarrhea
- Shaky limbs and trembling
- Headache and body aches

Anxiety grips the mind and locks it down, making it seem impossible to concentrate on the test material or remember what was studied. When that happens to your child, the emotional and behavioral signs of anxiety appear. Does your child have any of the following emotions during testing?

- Feeling overwhelmed
- Feeling helplessness, hopelessness
- Feeling shame and worthlessness, feels like a failure
- Feeling panic

Whether your child openly advertises her distress about testing or not, the following behaviors may occur before, during, or after testing, indicating test anxiety:

- Is unable to concentrate or freezes up during the test
- Cries or gets sad or depressed
- Complains about being sick
- Has angry outbursts or tantrums
- Gets exhausted, fatigued, or feels faint
- Has trouble falling asleep the night before a test or has insomnia

Children with test anxiety may rush through the test to stop the anxiety or give up and not even try to finish. They often withdraw from academic and social activities and may refuse to go to school. Some children with severe cases of test anxiety feel so much distress that they threaten to hurt themselves. Test anxiety blocks the ability of your child to achieve his academic potential, as well as undermines his social development.

What Are the Causes of Test Anxiety?

Test anxiety can be caused by a number of factors. Children who are worriers and anxious, already have an anxiety disorder, or are depressed when they enter school are at a higher risk of developing test anxiety. Their heightened sense of feelings and emotions and a tendency to overreact to the physical manifestations of the fight-or-flight response may cause them to overreact to test pressure. These children may also have low self-worth and cope poorly in stressful situations.

Students with learning disabilities that include dyslexia and attention-deficit disorders generally feel "different" from their peers as they struggle to keep up with class work. These children also have a high risk of developing test anxiety because of their difficulties in paying attention in class, learning new concepts, and being able to memorize information. Low self-confidence is a common characteristic found in students with learning disabilities. Children who are perfectionists may manifest test anxiety, because anything other than an A is a failure, so every test is fraught with anxiety to be perfect.

Other causes of test anxiety are life changes such as parental divorce, death of a family member or friend, moving to a new school, sibling rivalry, or becoming physically ill. School problems such as being bullied, being socially inept, and not getting along with the teacher are other causes of test anxiety. Practical reasons include having poor homework and study skills.

What Are the Short- and Long-Term Effects of Test Anxiety?

Children who have test anxiety suffer on a daily basis, because a test is always just around the corner. Even those students who get high scores in spite of their anxiety may experience chronic emotional distress. Some students blank out on tests because of their nerves, feel defeated, give up, and begin to underachieve. They may be placed in lower academic classes, feel ashamed, and isolate themselves from their peers and shun social activities. Long-term consequences include dropping out of school, being unable to reach one's potential, developing mental disorders such as depression and anxiety disorders, and using drugs and alcohol.

What Kinds of Tests Will My Child Have to Take?

Your child may take three different kinds of tests within one school year. Each type of test measures your child's knowledge or abilities in different ways. Classroom tests are given on specific subjects, like math or spelling, to determine how much your child has learned from class instruction, and where he might need help. These tests can be given weekly, monthly, or even daily. Standardized tests include the norm-referenced tests, such as the Iowa Test of Basic Skills, that measure a student's achievement against a sample of other students across the country in the same grade and rank students based on percentages. If your child ranks 80 percent, that means she has scored better than 80 percent of the students in her sample group. The last type of tests are the standardized-based tests that determine the progress of both student and school proficiency in major subjects. These tests are constructed by the state and school districts. Standardized tests may be given once a year or every few years depending on the state. For more information on standardized testing, see the resources list at the back of the book.

Your child will face continual testing throughout elementary and secondary school. Test anxiety can turn your child's school experience into a daily ordeal. However, test anxiety can be conquered, and the remainder of the chapter teaches you how to help your child do this.

Overcoming Test Anxiety Clinic

It is upsetting when your child brings home tests with low scores. If you have determined that your child can understand what is being taught but is suffering from test anxiety, then the following guidelines, exercises, and techniques will enable your child to become successful at test taking.

✎ Guidelines for Helping Your Child Overcome Test Anxiety

1. Talk to your child about tests: why they are given and how she feels about them. What are her fears about testing? That she will fail? That classmates or her teacher will think she is dumb? Listen to her and reassure her.

2. Do not yell at or demean your child for low test scores or allow others to do so.

3. Be clear about your expectations that she will study and try hard on tests, and that you will work with her on any problems that she has.

4. At the first sign of problems, contact the school and team up with the teacher for direction in helping your child to study, and for exemptions during testing, for example, taking the test in another room or giving more time. Assure your child that you are going to work together to help her to test well.

5. Have her wear comfortable clothing and have extra pencils, erasers, and so on.

6. Decide with your child where she is going to study for a test. Help her organize the study space and school materials. Teach her how to study—see the exercises beginning on the next page.

7. Limit TV and computer time. Find educational programs and other materials that reinforce the class work. Be a good role model: Make learning interesting and fun.

Also, explain to your child that a failing grade is not a catastrophe or an indication that she is "stupid"; it signals where she needs help. Stress her strengths and praise her efforts to build up her confidence. Learn to relax yourself and lower family stress. Make sure your child gets to sleep early the night before a test, eats a healthy breakfast, and gets affection and positive vibes from you that you know she will do her best.

Exercises: What You Need to Do and Have on Hand

Read through the exercise before you begin. The prerequisites are breathing (Chapter 14), being present and centered (Chapter 15), and letting go (Chapter 16). Have your "home classroom" ready with a desk and chair, along with mock tests and an alarm clock. For study rewards choose hugs and kisses, praise, healthy snacks, a short playtime, and so on. Determine how long each study segment will be, making it age appropriate. Start with a short time studying, five minutes on, five or ten minutes off, and gradually lengthen study time as your child's anxiety eases and confidence grows.

STUDYING IN BITS AND PIECES

Tell your child that she is going to learn how to study in little pieces of time so that she will not get as stressed about the test. Read the exercises in Chapter 7, "My Child Has Homework Anxiety," for additional information on how to talk to your child about managing the schoolwork load. If your child has something special she uses to "stay in the moment," have it on the desk.

1. Place all study materials on the table.
2. Have your child choose one sheet or page to study. Put all the rest away in a closet or another room. Tell her, "See, they don't exist anymore. You're only going to focus on one page at a time."
3. Have her belly breathe for a few minutes before starting.
4. Set an alarm clock for the desired study time and have her work until the alarm rings. If she gets anxious or her attention wanders, have her breathe, use body awareness, loosen and float, and so on until she can return to her work.

Continue until all studying is finished. Reward her appropriately in between study segments and after all the work is completed.

PRACTICING WITH MOCK TESTS

Make up a test from the work your child has studied, or get an old test from the teacher. Time her the exact time she will have in class to finish the exam.

1. Have your child practice walking into the home classroom while belly breathing, then going to her desk and sitting down.
2. You, "the teacher," say something like, "Okay class, I'm going to give out the test." Have your child continue to belly breathe while you walk to her and put the test on the desk.
3. Tell your child not to scan the test. Instead have her block out every question with her hands or pieces of paper (she will need permission from teacher for this) except number one. Tell her to remember that there is only number one in the moment; no other question exists. This will keep her anxiety at a manageable level.
4. Have her breathe and read the first question carefully. Tell her if she does not know it to block it out and move on to number two and so forth using breathing and other techniques to remain calm.
5. When she has finished, have her put her test down and you collect it.
6. Grade the paper, and then talk about what areas she needs help with.
7. Celebrate a job well done.

VISUALIZING TAKING A TEST

After your child has studied the test material, have her sit in a comfortable chair or lie down the night before the test. Have her belly breathe while you softly say, "See yourself going to school on test day; see yourself going into class and sitting down at your desk; see the teacher giving out the test; see yourself taking the test; feel all of the studying you did flow out of you—you know the answers; see yourself challenged by some answers, but they do not cause anxiety—you work them out or move on; see yourself completing the test well; see yourself handing in the test paper; see yourself feeling good about a job well done."

Be sure to review all of Chapters 4 and 5 for other exercises and techniques you can adapt to test taking. Explain to your child that learning how to ease test anxiety will take time and practice, and that doing well on tests is all about learning skills and strategies for studying and test taking. By working together and with the help of the school, she will succeed.

CHAPTER 9

My Child Is a Perfectionist

൭

M ANY CHILDREN STRIVE TO BE THE BEST AT EVERYTHING. Although that is a noble goal for these high achievers, other children cross the line on the road to success creating emotional havoc in major areas in their lives—they become perfectionists.

Jerry, a sixth grader, is so obsessed with getting everything "perfect" that he checks and double-checks homework, turning the one hour it would take to finish homework into an anxious and frustrating three-or-more-hour event, leaving him feeling angry at himself and stupid.

Charmaine, a fourth grader, feels that she must get 100 percent or an A on every homework assignment, test, and school project, and she usually does. She "must" be the top student all the time or she suffers anxiety, and she suffers most of the time because she worries continually that she won't make the grade. An A minus is not good enough; B, a disaster. The continual worry does not allow her to take pride in her accomplishments; she's never quite good enough. Perfectionism has taken the joy out of her life.

Second grader Luis wants everything to be perfect, too. By seven years of age, he has already lost his spontaneity about life, avoiding having new experiences as much as possible such as meeting new friends or trying new activities—he just can't take the risk of possi-

ble failure or of being disappointed in others. His expectations are so high for himself and others that he has negatively turned off his peer group.

Although their perfectionism takes different forms, Jerry, Charmaine, and Luis have one main feature in common: They are all suffering and are blocked from normal academic and social development. As a parent, it is imperative to understand the nature of perfectionism, how to respond to your child's belief that "I have to be perfect," and how to help him make positive changes in his thinking and actions.

What Is Perfectionism?

Children who are high achievers make teachers happy and parents proud. These students are self-motivated and generally interested in a broad range of activities in and outside of school. They strive for excellence, to be the best in all of their pursuits, from getting high grades to playing solo in the school orchestra to becoming a star athlete. If they don't hit their goals, they accept the fact, move on, and work smarter and harder. These children develop well academically and socially, and have successful school careers.

But other students take striving for achievement to new and dangerous heights, for they pursue perfection to their detriment. They don't strive for excellence that is achievable with hard work; they strive for perfection, which is impossible to attain. Becoming a perfectionist is to walk down a path that leads to anxiety, depression, obsession, compulsion, and ultimately failure.

Perfectionism is not considered a formal mental condition or disease. Rather, it is a mind-set where people set up ridiculously high standards that are impossible to meet while attempting to attain unreachable goals. No matter how hard they try, they can't win because they set themselves up to fail. Even if the perfectionist child achieves A's all the time, it's still not good enough. When the perfectionist child fails to reach her image of perfection, she will punish herself with critical self-talk, such as, "I always get things wrong," or "I'll never be as good as my classmates." These students trap themselves in a double-bind situation with no way out.

Perfectionist children are rigid in their thinking, which is called *dichotomous thinking*. Everything is black or white, good or bad, right or wrong. A task has to be completed perfectly and there is only one right way to do it. If that way does not work, then a failure has occurred. There are no grays in their world, no mistakes allowed, no options, which makes completing almost anything to their "standards" nightmarish and pretty impossible.

> *Gwen's kindergarten teacher asks the class to draw a square and color it in. Gwen, already a perfectionist, cannot complete the square because the first line she draws is not straight enough for her. Over and over, again and again, Gwen draws the line, then erases it, trying to get it perfect. With the rest of the class finished and waiting, Gwen is still only on the first line. Her teacher is trying to help move her along, but Gwen can't and her anxiety is increasing as the class looks on.*

Gifted children can have perfectionist traits and are often high achievers and want to excel, but perfectionism can also lead to procrastination, underachievement, and defiance about going to school, doing homework, and studying. Perfectionism is rated on a continuum: Some children seek perfection in some areas, such as academics or sports, but not in other areas of their lives. Others have traits of perfectionism, but that doesn't hold them back in succeeding in school and socially. There are some children, though, whose entire life is ruled by their attempt to be perfect, which creates daily suffering and stunts their social and academic development.

Is My Child a Perfectionist?

Children who operate under the heavy weight of perfectionism will experience chronic physical and emotional symptoms and exhibit certain types of behaviors, such as the following:

- Have high levels of tension and anxiety.
- Be rigid and controlling, obsessive-compulsive.
- Be afraid to take risks or to try new things; be terrified of failing.
- Have low self-worth; compare themselves negatively to others.
- Ignore accomplishments.
- Find it difficult to start or finish assignments.
- Are not content or happy; are depressed.
- Expect family members and friends to live up to the same ideals and are critical when they can't do so.
- Have difficulty in forming close relationships.

If your child gets straight A's and is involved in school activities but has perfectionist tendencies, he may be as unhappy as a child who is failing in school. Although his grades are good and he socializes, he may still be dealing with stress about being perfect and will need help to learn how to handle life differently.

Perfectionist Self-Talk

Another clue to your child's perfectionism are the words and phrases she uses to describe herself. Look for descriptions like these: "I always fail." "I'm fat." "I'm ugly." "I never get asked to play." "I'm stupid." "I should have tried harder." "I have to get 100 percent on my tests." "I can't do the work." "No one likes me." "I'm the only one who has to study this hard." "My teacher thinks I'm stupid." It is exhausting and disheartening listening to this verbal self-abuse. Imagine how the child who beats herself up on a daily basis with this type of talk feels. That's why perfectionist children are often depressed and tired.

Why Does My Child Procrastinate?

Procrastination is the conscious act of putting off an action or a task to a later time and it is something we all do, sometimes. Procrastination becomes a problem when it develops into chronic behavior, and the act of delaying results in negative consequences. Procrastination is a major symptom in perfectionist children and is driven by their fear of failure, all-or-nothing thinking, and the mind-set that there is only one right way to do a task.

> *Sheri is a fifth grader who almost never does her homework assignments because she fears getting the work wrong. Her anxiety would get very high right before she would start, because she believed that her writing had to look a certain way. If it didn't, then everything was wrong and had to be rewritten. It could take hours to do even a little of the work because she would cry or get angry and then refuse to do it. The perfectionism overwhelmed her. Every school night was full of tension and fighting with her parents, so now Sheri tells them either "I have no homework," or "I finished it in school." What she has really started doing is throwing out the homework in the garbage before she gets home. Now, she is failing almost every subject.*

Children who are perfectionists will put off beginning assignments or find it impossible to complete a task because they fear that they cannot reach perfection. Not being perfect devastates them, negatively reinforcing feelings of being a loser and a failure. Helping perfectionist children to overcome the distorted view they have of themselves, and the world around them, is crucial to their mental and physical health.

What Are the Negative Effects of Perfectionism?

Perfectionism is a complex condition that begins in childhood. The consequences of attempting to live life to an imagined exacting standard causes feelings of guilt and shame because the perfectionist *never* feels good about how he has done something. Low confidence and self-worth are common because perfectionists always feel like failures. Feeling sad and down for a majority of the day is common because perfectionists can never reach their goal of perfection. Perfectionists are rigid in their thinking and unbending in their behaviors about how things should be done, which could lead to obsessive-compulsive tendencies, such as the excessive need to control things, and to mental disorders such as eating disorders. The ability to set goals and strive to achieve them is often stifled by perfectionism because of the fear of failure. A perfectionist is doomed to failure before the task is even begun. Children who are perfectionists are at risk of developing serious mental conditions such as depression, anxiety disorders, and eating disorders.

Why Is My Child a Perfectionist?

The answer to this question is far from perfect because no one knows exactly why a child becomes a perfectionist, but several theories exist. Biological theories point to the personality traits or temperament that children are born with. Perfectionist characteristics of children can be seen early on. For example, some children are controlling about their environment—they keep their rooms clean and every toy has its place—whereas other kids could care less.

Parenting style and demands of parents have been shown to contribute to perfectionism, by having children always trying to please parents, seeking parental approval, but never being able to get it. Parents who are perfectionists themselves will deliver the message to their children that nothing is ever good enough. For example, "Oh, you got a B plus. Well we want to see an A next time." Perfectionist parents praise their child less, and can stifle their child's motivation to learn and have his own ideas and teach him to be afraid to make mistakes.

Major life changes or traumatic experiences make a child feel unstable, unsafe, and out of control. Becoming a perfectionist feels like a way to take back control. A child facing a world that feels unsafe can take charge by putting a rigid structure into place in his small world. For the perfectionist child, everything has to be just so or severe emotional discomfort and anxiety will result.

Cultural norms and behaviors are an aspect of the development of perfectionism. Children live in a competitive world where either only the end result is celebrated or what society deems as worthy is the accepted goal. Parents and teachers give praise for getting all A's, making the touchdown, being the most popular student, being pretty, or winning the spelling bee. If effort does not pay off, or if a child's uniqueness does not fit the norm, praise for a job well done or positive reinforcement may not be given enough weight, or not given at all.

What Treatments Are Available for My Child?

If perfectionism is standing in the way of your child's ability to function well, intervention and treatment are recommended. Two types of therapy are commonly used for treating perfectionism: cognitive-behavioral therapy (CBT) and psychodynamic psychotherapy. In both, therapists begin with helping children to become aware of their perfectionism, to understand how trying to live up to impossible standards negatively impacts their life, and learn how to make positive changes.

In CBT, the therapist helps clients to see that their thinking is distorted and destructive, and teaches them how to change thought patterns and eventually their attitudes and beliefs about themselves and others. Psychodynamic psychotherapy explores the root causes of perfectionist behavior, helps clients to become aware of and embrace the positive qualities about themselves, and helps clients to make changes in their thought patterns.

Finding a mental health professional to treat your child is important, but that alone is not enough. It is also important to make changes in how you parent, and in how your family interrelates to end the cycle of perfectionism.

Overcoming Perfectionism Clinic

Trying to get a child to give up perfectionist thinking and behavior is not easy. You know that you can't convince your child to not worry about getting an A all the time or to "relax and just do your best, that's good enough." The rigid, obsessive thinking of a perfectionist trumps parental reassurance. You can learn, however, to respond in ways that will be beneficial to your child and can teach her how to give up the debilitating perfectionism. The guidelines and exercises in this section can help you.

✎ Guidelines for Helping Your Child

1. Educate yourself about perfectionism.
2. Observe your child, yourself, and other family members for perfectionist thinking and behaviors. Do you unconsciously model perfectionism to your child in what you say and do? If so, get help to change yourself.
3. If you demand perfection, change your message to "strive for excellence." Be flexible, not rigid.
4. When your child completes a task, stop yourself from redoing it to make it "perfect." Your child is not an adult and can't live up to your adult standards—that comes with growth.
5. Teach your child that mistakes are part of life and everybody makes them. Help her to handle failures in positive, healthy ways.
6. Praise your child for her efforts in doing her best even if she comes in last.
7. Do not base your love on your child's achievement—separate it from a task well done.
8. Help your child to take risks even if she fears failure. The lesson is that nothing is perfect, there is no guarantee no matter what you do, and you can be uncomfortable with disappointment but still go forward.

Another way to help your child is to talk about your own disappointments and failures, that you went on regardless, and how and what you learned from the experience. Also, do not judge others in front of your child or point out their flaws—teach your child acceptance of self and others. Your child is getting a constant barrage of cultural messages of perfection on TV, the Internet, and from their peers. Counteract these negative images and ideas with your own positive take on the importance of accepting his own humanness and that of others.

Learning to Make Mistakes

Perfectionism is pervasive, coloring every aspect of your child's life. The exercises in this chapter will most likely cause your child to become anxious, so be patient and move slowly. These are counterconditioning exercises. Tell your child that the exercises will help her to feel relaxed and calm while making mistakes, ease the obsessive-compulsive behavior of redoing work, and accept that mistakes are part of learning and being human. Routine practice is crucial for success. Keep practice times short, with gradual increases in time imagining mistakes, as your child's anxiety decreases and confidence grows.

Prerequisites are knowing how to breathe (Chapter 14), being able to stay in the moment (Chapter 15), and knowing how to let go and float (Chapter 16). Talk to your child's teacher and other school personnel to enlist their help. You will need a timer.

First, with your child make a list of what mistakes to work on first. Rate each fear on the School Anxiety Scale in Chapter 16. After the list is made, decide which is the least anxiety-producing situation, and start with that. For example:

- I'm afraid to color outside the lines in class. Scale rating: 9
- I'm afraid to color outside the lines in my homework. Scale rating: 6
- I'm afraid of getting arithmetic problems wrong. Scale rating: 7
- I'm afraid that my clothes, hair, or any part of my appearance is not perfect and the kids in my class will laugh at me. Scale rating: 10

With younger children, it may be easier for them to express themselves through play instead of writing a list. You may wish to adapt the exercise, "Variation: Using the Tangible Feared Scene," found in Chapter 16, "Learning to Let Go and Flow." If you are a perfectionist, practice the exercises for yourself first.

IMAGINING MAKING MISTAKES

1. Choose one mistake that your child will imagine making. Have your child lie down or sit in a comfortable chair with her eyes closed. Tell her that she may become very anxious

when she pictures herself making mistakes, but that she knows how to relax herself, and you are right there with her. Set the timer for two to three minutes.

2. Have her imagine herself making the mistake over and over again. Rate her anxiety on the scale.

3. Have her begin belly breathing and loosen her body. Say to her, "Relax your head, neck, and shoulders; relax your back and chest; relax your arms, hands, and fingers; relax your legs, feet, and toes." Repeat until she relaxes.

4. Tell her to continue to imagine making the mistake while breathing and loosening. Now, either you say or have her say aloud, "I can make this mistake and nothing will happen to me." Repeat this five to ten times.

5. As she continues picturing herself making the mistake, tell her to calm herself more by using body awareness techniques in Chapter 15 and the Letting Go and Floating exercise in Chapter 16.

6. If she cannot relax or becomes upset, tell her to stop thinking about making the mistake, praise her effort, and return to the loosening exercise. If she was able to ease her anxiety even a little, have her rate it on the anxiety scale to show her that she can control her feelings.

7. When you are finished, ask her how she feels.

Making Mistakes for Real

Once your child can imagine making mistakes and is able to calm down and relax quickly, it is time to practice in real situations. This will be hard for her to do, so be patient and understanding. Tell her that you know she wants to do well in school, but that planning to make small mistakes is only an exercise to help her feel less anxious. Assure her that you are not asking her to fail, but to learn how to handle mistakes in a positive way. If your child gets frightened at the thought of doing this part of the exercise, she is not ready, so don't push her. Instead, tell her it is okay and continue practicing the other relaxation exercises or Imagining Making Mistakes until she is ready to try again.

This is a good time to contact her teacher and guidance counselor if you haven't done so already to get their cooperation, ideas, and feedback. You want them to reassure her, too, that it is okay to make mistakes in her homework and in class. Assure your child that none of her classmates will know what is going on. Together, create a plan of action. Write down which mistakes she plans to make, and what exercises she wants to use to calm herself. After she makes the mistake, follow up by asking her how she felt about it and what happened. Use fourth grader Scott's example below as a guideline:

> "I plan to purposely do three math problems wrong on my homework and hand it in. The techniques I will use are belly breathing and body awareness." What happened? "I got very nervous when I had to write down the wrong answers and felt bad about myself when the teacher collected the homework. I started to call myself stupid again, but I was able to stop that. I did feel bad when I got the homework back and had three wrong answers, but I'd practiced imagining doing this at home, so I knew how to calm myself."

Other examples of planned mistakes include misspelling words; saying in class, "I don't know the answer," when she really does; answering wrong on a test; playing the wrong note on a musical instrument; doing homework and not checking it over; being late for an event; or making a mess in the house and not cleaning it up right away.

Two other features of perfectionism that require attention are the negative attitude your child carries around about himself and others and the negative self-talk, that critical voice that runs through his head making him feel bad. Exercises for those aspects of perfectionism will be found at the end of Chapter 10, "Building Your Child's Self-Esteem."

The exercises in this chapter are very difficult to follow through with. Ideally, you want to have the cooperation of the school. If the school won't give it and your child wants to try it anyway, have your child make very small mistakes imperceptible to the school or practice making mistakes that have nothing to do with schoolwork. Young children may not be able to tolerate the feelings generated by making mistakes for real, and even older children may be afraid to try. At least have your child practice the Imagining Making Mistakes exercise, because overcoming perfectionism is crucial to healthy emotional development and living a happy and rewarding life.

CHAPTER 10

Building Your Child's Self-Esteem

∾

Throughout the book, many reasons for why children develop school anxiety have been discussed such as separation anxiety, test anxiety, and bullying. One constant in all of the reasons are the feelings and beliefs children have about themselves, their world and their place in it, their uniqueness, their self-image, and their self-esteem.

Kari, in fifth grade, has suffered from school anxiety since kindergarten. She was diagnosed with separation anxiety when she first entered school, and although Kari has adjusted to some degree since then, school is not a happy place for her. She is dyslexic, and even though she likes the small classes she attends in the resource room, she feels "stupid," that she is not "normal" like the other kids. Kari is also overweight and has been teased about it. Kari's sense of herself makes her unhappy a good deal of the time. She also avoids actively participating in class or school activities, and challenging herself such as auditioning for the school play, although she dreams about becoming an actress. Kari makes no attempt at school friendships because she fears rejection.

This chapter defines self-esteem and its effect on school performance and gives guidelines and exercises for aiding parents and schools to help children build strong, healthy identities and to thrive in school and in life.

What Is Self-Esteem?

Self-esteem is a concept that has been on the psychological radar since William James, an American psychologist and philosopher, coined the term in 1890. Over the decades, many interpretations and definitions of self-esteem have emerged, but simply put, self-esteem in children is how they feel about themselves; how they feel about the expectations of parents and family members, friends, and other important people in their lives; and how these people and the world at large react and respond to them.

Self-esteem is a complex combination of elements whose development begins in early childhood, and continues throughout the life span. Having high self-esteem includes the capability to handle life's challenges, to feel accepted and worthy, to interact well socially, to find purpose in life and achieve goals, to have values, and to be loved and give love.

All people carry around a mental picture of who they think they are, called self-image, which is made up of their strengths, weaknesses, abilities, and qualities. It is this mental image of himself that a child carries that will have a major impact on his success in elementary school, later in adolescence, and into adulthood. The words *self-worth* and *self-esteem* are used interchangeably in this chapter.

How Does Self-Esteem Develop?

From babyhood on, self-esteem develops as part of the framework of a child's blossoming identity. When parents respond lovingly to a baby's cries with smiles and other nurturing behaviors, the child learns to feel loved and cherished. As a child grows and goes out into the world, not only parents and family members but other people such as friends, teachers, and classmates will react to, evaluate, judge, and mirror their feelings toward the child about all sorts of things, such as personality, behavior, physical looks, interests, and race. What form these responses take will go a long way in creating the foundation for the development of either high or low self-esteem. Temperament, the innate characteristics that a child is born with such as shyness, boldness, introversion, extroversion, and risk taking, also plays a role in the development of self-esteem.

Self-esteem is not rigid, for it grows and develops along with your child's maturation and life experiences, successes, and failures. And your child's self-esteem may be high in some instances and low in others, for example, feeling confident and outgoing at home with family and friends, but shy and withdrawn with classmates. Or feeling confident in reading, but insecure about math. As a parent, you play the most important role in building the foundation of your child's self-esteem. Maybe you are saying to yourself, "I have no idea how to help my child with this." Later in the chapter you will find guidelines and exercises to help your child have a healthy self-image.

What Are the Causes of Low Self-Esteem?

The reasons behind the development of low self-esteem are complex, based on many factors. Some of the causes are discussed next.

Parenting Style

The connection between a child's self-esteem and parental behavior has been a field of study since the 1920s. In the 1990s, Diana Baumrind, along with other researchers, described four types of parenting styles and examined parental attitudes about child rearing that included the ways parents think and behave, how they respond to children, and what they demand of them. These studies also looked at how these styles impact children's emotional development.

Authoritarian parents are strict, controlling, and demanding. House rules are clear, but are rigid and inflexible. These parents are generally aloof and unresponsive to the child's emotional needs and do not allow for the discussion of problems. Consequences for bad behavior are often punitive and sometimes harsh, such as yelling, name-calling, and hitting.

Indulgent/permissive/nondirective parents are warm, accepting, and undemanding. They set no clear rules, offer little guidance, do not create a family structure, and put few limits on the child's behavior with no consequences for bad behavior. They are usually responsive to the child's emotions.

Authoritative parents are loving and accepting and do set clear rules about what is and what is not acceptable behavior. Consequences are consistent but not harsh and are meant to teach a child responsibility and how to control behavior. A child is taught how to express emotions in healthy ways.

Uninvolved parents respond very little to a child's needs, and there are few demands or rules and almost no family structure of any kind. In the severe form of this type of parenting, the parents are considered rejecting and neglectful.

So, how might children be impacted by parenting style? Children with authoritarian parents may have low self-esteem because they are not allowed to have choices, make decisions, or express themselves. They may become followers or act out, or they may do well academically but have a hard time relating to and playing with others. Indulgent/permissive parenting leads to children who are used to getting their own way. Children with little or no structure may have tantrums outside the home, and lack discipline and self-control, which are necessary for academic and social success. Children whose parents are uninvolved and neglectful are at a high risk of having low self-esteem and of performing poorly in school. An authoritative parenting style allows children to develop confidence through having choices, making decisions, being accountable for behavior, and having the right to emotional and creative expression.

Children who are abused verbally, emotionally, physically, and sexually or traumatized in some way have an almost impossible task of developing high self-worth and the ability to cope successfully in life—although some do. Children whose parents argue a lot or who are addicted to alcohol or drugs, gambling, shopping, work, or computers are also at risk of developing poor identities.

Don't let this information make you feel like you have been doing "everything" wrong! The most important thing to remember about being a parent is that parenting happens on a continuum, authoritarian on one end, uninvolved or abusive on the other. Most of us are somewhere in the middle but could move back and forth between extremes, too. Your responses to your child may be more demanding one day and less the next. Sometimes you will give too much, sometimes not enough. You will make mistakes as a parent. You're human, right? It is a good idea to examine your parental skills, see what's working and what needs work—then hone these skills so you can learn how best to guide your child to become happy and the best he can be.

Loss of a Parent

Losing a parent is a devastating event for children, turning their stable world into frightening chaos. Divorce, death of a parent, mental or physical illness of a parent, or abandonment leave children feeling rejected and hopeless. Children whose home life is disrupted by this type of loss generally have emotional challenges that will affect the development of their self-esteem.

Negative School and Social Experience

Being bullied; having a learning, physical, or mental disability; being frightened and anxious about tests, class work, or speaking up in class, or about anything related to school will impact a child's attitude about his intelligence, personality, capability, and ultimately his self-worth. Having a hard time making and keeping friends and being excluded from social interaction with peers in and out of school creates feelings and beliefs in children that something is wrong with them or that they are not worthy. Children who are different in any way, including being overweight or underweight, not pretty or handsome in the expected cultural sense, poor if they attend a school in an upscale neighborhood, or a member of a race in the minority in the area or school, may be teased, bullied, excluded, and related to differently not only by peers but by teachers and school staff, too, which could affect their self-image.

Does My Child Have Low Self-Esteem?

Children often have a tough time expressing how they feel about things that are going wrong for them or that worry them. Children who have low self-esteem and are struggling in school often feel helpless, hopeless, and alone in their situation—they can't see a way out or a means to change the situation. Other children may be unaware, confused, or frightened of their feelings, and act out their emotions in any of the following behaviors:

- Feels depressed, anxious, and withdrawn
- Refuses to go to school or complains about not feeling well on school mornings
- Avoids or gives up easily on schoolwork, exhibits frustration when having to solve a difficult problem, or shows little participation in class
- Has test and homework anxiety
- Has trouble making and keeping friends, or avoids socializing altogether
- Exhibits aggressive behavior toward family, friends, or school personnel
- Uses negative self-talk with phrases such as "I'm stupid," "I can't learn this," or "Nobody likes me"

Your child will most likely exhibit some of these behaviors at some point in response to difficult or frustrating situations. Growing up is indeed hard to do at times. But it is the frequency or chronic behavior that will alert you to the fact that your child has a problem and that you need to take action to avoid the consequences of low self-esteem.

What Are the Consequences of Low Self-Esteem?

The short-term consequences of low self-esteem for children in elementary school include the obvious one that low self-esteem creates problems in social, intellectual, and emotional development and makes navigating the school environment at times extremely difficult. It can also lead to the development of mental conditions such as an anxiety disorder, depression, or social anxiety. The long-term effects that extend into adolescence and even adulthood include eating disorders, teenage pregnancy, job and career problems, and difficulties with inter-personal relationships, and when low self-esteem is severe, suicidal be-havior.

Overcoming Low Self-Esteem Clinic

Okay, you've determined that your child is insecure in certain areas and this is causing him some pain and suffering, and you are afraid of the long-lasting effect on his future. So, sit down, breathe, and relax. There are many ways to help your child feel good about himself, and you are on the right track for doing so.

Take a Hard Look in the Mirror

First, make an honest assessment of yourself. Are you insecure? Do you, your partner, or spouse have low self-esteem? If so, you have to work on that. Remember you are the most powerful force in how your child sees himself and develops, and in how he relates to the greater world. Start making changes today; what you say and how you act are extremely important. For example, stop saying things to either yourself or aloud like, "I'm so stupid," "I can't learn these things," or "I'm fat." Stop having meltdowns in front of your child when life throws you a curveball. Model to your child that you are capable of handling any-thing that comes your way. This will teach him how to roll with the punches and will build his confidence. Children want a strong, fair, and loving parent. That makes them feel safe and sound. Get profes-sional help for yourself if necessary.

Fully Accept Your Child

Next, think about your child—her personality, characteristics, and quirks. How do you relate to her or interact with her? How does she relate to you, family members, friends, teachers, classmates, and other important people in her life? Be honest about your expectations of her. Are you disappointed if she is not the A student, athlete, beauty, or social butterfly you'd hoped for? Are you envious of other parents whose children are considered "stars"? Do you feel embarrassed as a parent if your child has a learning, emotional, or physical disability? Does this make you feel unworthy as a parent? Sometimes are you resentful that your child has problems?

These are tough questions, but you have to answer them candidly because your child knows how you feel about her and her problems, even if you think you are hiding it from her or you're not conscious of your true feelings. These questions have nothing to do with loving your child—that's a given. But feelings equal behavior, and even subtle negative messages from you such as facial tension or an eye roll will impact your child. The more aware you become of how you truly feel about your child in a given moment, the better you can take control of your behavior, and positively change it.

Make an effort to view and treat your child as a distinctive being and do not compare her to her siblings, classmates, or other children. Show her that you love her unconditionally, not based on what she has done or not done. One of the most important jobs of parenting is to guide your child into the school and social world at her own pace respecting her unique qualities.

✎ Guidelines for Building Your Child's Self-Esteem

1. Listen to and accept your child's feelings.
2. Do not harshly criticize, make fun of, or demean your child as he struggles with his problems, or allow anyone else to do so.
3. Use realistic praise for efforts and accomplishments.
4. Set clear and specific age-appropriate rules and expectations.
5. Allow your child to find his own way in new situations, and encourage him to keep trying when he is challenged.
6. Give him responsibilities at home that fit his age skills— guide him into independence.
7. Learn how to use discipline in a positive, nonjudgmental way and be fair and consistent about it—talk about the behavior, not his character.
8. Show interest in what captivates him, in his schoolwork and

creative play. Show that you are proud of him by telling him so and displaying his work.

Teach your child how to handle failures and disappointments by learning from them and accepting life's limitations; don't always rescue him. Also teach him how to make decisions. Discuss problems with him, brainstorm, and respect his opinions. If self-esteem issues revolve around schoolwork or situations, meet with teachers and other pertinent school personnel.

The following are self-esteem-building exercises.

FINDING THE POSITIVES

You will need a list of your child's strengths, interests, positive characteristics, and so on; scrapbook or photo album; photos of your child at different ages, with family and friends while he is playing and doing things he loves to do, and his accomplishments; cutouts of positive words, statements, phrases, and poems that apply; pictures from magazines of things that are special to your child, such as animals, trucks, someone singing or playing a musical instrument; crayons, colored pencils, and paints; and adhesive material.

First, find a quiet place alone and write down all of your child's attributes, talents, positive features, and characteristics. These are not ranked in any way; after all, liking art or music, or loving people or animals is as worthy as being an A student in math or reading or excelling in athletics. Put the list away.

Now, explain to your child that together you are going to create an album that shows him why he is special, smart, creative, and so on. With him, choose a name for the album, such as "Paul's Positive Scrapbook." Tell him that this book is private between you and him unless he wishes to show it to someone. Next, have him write down, or write for him, what he thinks his strengths and positive characteristics are. Then tell him what you wrote about him earlier.

Together begin to create his album following his list and adding new things as he thinks of them. If he wishes, he can add items from your list too. Let his creativity flow as he pastes, draws, paints, and writes in his book. As the scrapbook grows, he will have a visible picture book with proof of the things that make him special and unique. He can take it out and look at in good times, and in bad times when he feels low about himself. With your child, add photos, positive statements, and artwork to the album as often as possible.

FINDING THE POSITIVES: VARIATION

Say to your child that you are going to teach him how to use his scrapbook to make himself feel good in school when he gets anxious. Have him choose a favorite page in his scrapbook. Ask him how he feels when he looks at the page: happy, confident, strong, safe, creative? Now, have him sit in a chair while looking at his favorite page for one minute. Then ask him to close his eyes, belly breathe, and imagine the favorite page for one minute. Can he picture the page in his mind? Does it make him feel good? Repeat imagining three more times. Now, have him keep his eyes open, belly breathe, and think about the page. Ask him how he feels. With practice, he will actually be able to concentrate on what is going on around him while thinking about "the page" to lower his anxiety. Have him practice with eyes open and eyes closed every day for a few weeks, then three times a week. Ask him to use this mental exercise during homework, testing, being called on in class, socializing, or any stress-filled situation.

Self-Talk

Self-talk is the internal dialogue that runs through our minds, all day long. It is generally unconscious and can be either positive or negative in nature. Self-talk is enormously powerful, affecting our feelings and behavior. If your child says to herself, "I always do poorly on math tests no matter how much I study," she is less likely to do well than a child who says, "I studied hard, know I can work the problems, and will do my best." Attitude is everything!

A child with low self-esteem will engage in negative self-talk, which over time could become automatic and habitual, and could destroy her confidence in both academic and social arenas. The good news is that negative self-talk can be turned off, and positive self-talk can be turned on.

TURNING ON POSITIVE SELF-TALK

For a week, carefully listen to how your child talks about herself, especially when she is challenged with schoolwork or social situations. Write down what she says. Explain self-talk using those examples. Tell her that you are going to teach her how to feel good about herself by having her change the negative things she says to herself into positives.

Have your child write, or you write for her, negative things that she says about herself, and share your observations with her, too. For example, she may say things like, "I can't try out for the school play because I know they won't pick me," or "I can never figure out the social studies homework and always get a zero." With her, write down positive statements that directly oppose the negative ones, such as, "I will try out for the play. I have as good a chance as anyone else," or "I can take the time to figure out the social studies homework, or ask for help."

Positive statements (see the samples in the previous paragraph) begin with an "I," are personal present-centered, and must have meaning and power to override the negative mental chatter. Make a list of negative statements, then opposing positive ones, and have your child repeat the positive statements for a few minutes each day. Also, teach her to become aware when she is putting herself down, and how changing to positive thinking will make her feel good about herself.

Doing Schoolwork with Fido

A number of years ago, schools and libraries initiated programs in which children read out loud for about twenty minutes to a therapy dog. The presence of these nonjudgmental canines resulted in benefits that include an increase in reading skills and comprehension, leading to increases in self-esteem, gains in social confidence, and a lesson in how to properly behave with animals.

You can check with your local library for information on this program, volunteer to create a Fido reading program in your school or library, or do a program at home. If you have a dog who will lie still, or better yet, sleep, or another pet such as a fish, bird, hamster, or other small caged animal (most cats won't cut it), have your child read aloud to the pet for a short time depending on the child's age and ability. Gradually increase reading time as your child's skills and confidence improve. Also, have your child practice spelling words to his pet, read back homework assignments and class notes, and study aloud for tests.

◌◌

Tackling your child's low self-esteem will take time, but it is an achievable goal. One of the most important ways to build your child's self-worth is to spend time with him. Take a walk, talk and listen, be silly together, create something, play games, or plan family outings. Show your child that you find joy in being with him. Show him that you go after your dreams, that you know how to cope with disappointments and hardships by taking positive action, that you are a responsible and responsive parent, and that you find joy in living, and he will gladly follow your lead. Additional resources for learning how to build a healthy self-image in your child are listed in the resources section of this book.

CHAPTER 11

My Child Is Being Bullied

ᕱᓚ

ULLYING IS A COMMON PROBLEM IN SCHOOLS. AT ONE TIME, IT
was thought to be just a normal part of growing up. Now bullying
is seen for what it is—a form of violence, and one of the leading
causes of school anxiety. For most children, school is a good safe place
where they make friends, learn new things, and begin to become aware
of their abilities and talents. But for a child who is being bullied, school
can turn into a daily nightmare. From physical attacks to isolation to
name-calling, bullying will cause its victim extreme stress and high
anxiety.

*Howie, a second grader, goes to a special class for reading, which
makes him feel "dumb" compared to his regular classmates. This
year a boy in his class called him a "dickhead" during recess in
front of the other boys in his class, who joined in laughing at him
and name calling until Howie ran away. Howie was devastated.
Now every day Howie is taunted either on the school bus, in the
school yard, or in the classroom, where the boys sometimes whisper
their taunts to him so the teacher can't overhear them. Howie feels
sick every school morning and his grades are dropping.*

*Keisha, a fifth grader, was best friends with three other girls since
kindergarten, but this year things changed. Her friends became
interested in clothes, tried to attract boys' attention, and giggled
about which boys they think are cute. They also started bullying a
new girl at school, making fun of her hairstyle. Keisha feels lost*

because she has other interests such as playing the violin in the school orchestra, and being part of the girl's softball team, activities they once shared with her but have dropped out of. She tried to hang out with them, but when she obviously didn't fit in and wouldn't participate in the bullying, they turned on her. Now they either make fun of her clothes or that she plays violin, or they avoid her, even telling her she can't sit with them at lunch because she is "weird." Keisha feels anxious every day in school not knowing what these girls will say, and sad that she has lost her friends. Her parents tell her to make new friends, but Keisha doesn't know where to begin.

Peter, a fourth grader, loves school, is in the gifted program, and is a math and science whiz. He has a few friends in the gifted program, but otherwise does not socialize with classmates. Instead he plays with kids in his neighborhood. Recently, a fifth-grade boy, known as one of the school bullies, pushed Peter around, twisted his arm, and stole his lunch money, saying he would beat Peter up if he told anyone about what happened, and wanted more money the next day. Peter was terrified and thought things could get worse if he told his parents or a teacher, because this bully has never been stopped from terrorizing other students. Peter has become nervous and distracted, his grades have slipped, and he wants to stay home from school on many mornings. When his parents question him, he gets angry at them and lashes out.

The form bullying takes is irrelevant to how much the victim suffers. The repeated threats, intimidation, humiliation, and isolation are constants in any type of bullying. This chapter will define bullying and discuss all of its aspects. Included are parental guidelines, how schools can help, and what actions you can take to help your child.

What Is Bullying?

Bullying is serious. It is intentional, unprovoked, aggressive, repeated physical or mental attacks on another student who is perceived as powerless and defenseless against the abuse. Bullying can be carried out by a single student or by a group of students against one student or a group of students. Sometimes the bullying is sporadic, and it could even be directed at friends, but in its most severe form, it is chronic and unending for the victim. This chronic form of bullying is considered antisocial behavior, leading to short- and long-term negative consequences for victims and perpetrators: development of conduct disorders in bullies, leading to adulthood antisocial problems; and lasting trauma for victims, the most severe reactions culminating in suicide or in homicide, such as is seen in the spate of school shootings by bullied students.

U.S. Government research groups, as well as other world organizations studying bullying, report that over 70 percent of all schoolchildren report having been the victim of a bullying incident. Some research shows that as children enter middle school, overt attacks peak, but decrease in high school, although verbal insults and isolation seem to remain constant in all grades. Other studies indicate that in elementary school, where it all begins, children are more likely to be bullied in direct forms, such as shoving and name-calling, than in higher grades.

What Are the Forms of Bullying?

The behaviors of bullying take many forms and are either overt and direct or hidden and secretive. All forms are devastating to the victim.

- *Physical*—kicking, shoving, hitting, punching, slapping, hair pulling, inappropriate touching, pulling pants down/skirt up, imprisoning in closet/locker, forcing victim to eat or drink something disgusting, stealing money, destroying victim's property
- *Verbal*—name-calling, teasing, taunting, making threats, ridiculing, spreading rumors/gossip, making racial or homophobic insults
- *Social*—isolating; shunning; excluding; harassing through e-mails, phone calls, or notes

The Internet age has opened the door to a new form of social harassment called "cyber-bullying," which is a deadly form of bullying done on social networking sites such as Facebook and MySpace. Not only are insults, name-calling, and threats open to the whole school to read at any time, but they could remain there throughout the child's entire school years, perpetuating the victim's isolation and fear. Children also receive threats and insults through instant messaging and text messaging on their cell phones.

The Dynamics of Bullying

Bullying has a wider effect than just its direct victims. Children who are not bullied themselves but who witness bullying on a daily basis are, along with the victim, at a higher risk of disliking school; wanting to stay home; and having stress-related conditions, such as anxiety and depression.

And it may take a village to victimize some students and allow bullying to continue because besides the lone bully, other students play an important role, too, as bystanders: those students who help the bully; students who watch and egg on the bully; students who avoid getting involved for fear they will be targeted too. An important element of bullying is that many victims become bullies themselves or join groups that bully. These children may displace their anger and frustration at the bully, and turn on a powerless classmate. Or, they may bully to fit in or to stop from being bullied themselves.

Schools play a role, too, if they do not have a zero-tolerance antibullying policy in place. Most schools do not tolerate physical bullying but do nothing about the covert forms it can take, such as name-calling and social and cyber isolation. To be effective, antibullying programs must include teaching all school personnel, students, and parents how to join together to stop bullying. If schools can put into place zero-tolerance weapons policies, where even a penknife accidentally left in a book bag from a family camping trip can bring on a suspension, then surely all forms of bullying can be addressed, too.

Although a student is not a bully target, living in a school environment where bullying is a daily occurrence will have a negative effect on the student. Students' mental and physical well-being, and their capacity to learn and grow socially, are both interrelated with their school environment.

Who Are the Bullies?

Both genders bully, although their styles are generally different. For the most part, boys physically attack, while girls use isolation, exclusion, and rumors. Bullies come from every racial and social economic background, and each bully is, of course, a unique individual, but they seem to have some common characteristics:

- Need for power and control
- No conscience about making others suffer and enjoying it
- No development of deep friendships or connections with others
- Inflated self-esteem
- Poor communication and conflict resolution skills

Chronic bullies are likely to demonstrate defiant behavior toward teachers, parents, and other adults. They often act out in school and at home and have a hard time obeying rules; many are poor students. Bullies may have been bullied themselves at one time or felt rejected by more popular students. Although bullies don't develop real friendships, they often become popular to some students and may be respected by classmates for their actions, perhaps mirroring the culture that power and celebrity are revered in any form. Decades of research into aggressive childhood behavior also suggests that some children are susceptible to the violence on TV and in the media and act it out in real life.

What If My Child Is a Bully?

If you find out that your child is a bully, you must act immediately. Bullying that continues could lead to long-term academic, social, and mental health problems. First, question your child about what is going on in school. Is he being bullied, or was he bullied? What else is there about school that may be bothering him? Tell him that bullying is unacceptable in any way, shape, or form, and that he will be held responsible for his actions. If he has school problems, tell him you both will work on solving them.

Take a hard look at your family life. Is there conflict, tension, arguing, or physical fighting? What is your parenting style? Does it lack structure? Is physical punishment or yelling the mode of discipline? How do you handle problems and emotions? How does your child? Bullying is learned behavior, but it can be unlearned and replaced with appropriate behaviors, such as good impulse control, communication skills, and empathy. To help your child stop bullying, talk to his teacher and guidance counselor to form a plan of action. If he continues, get counseling for him and your family as soon as possible.

Who Are the Victims?

Victims of bullying seem to have many common traits that bullies seize on to allow them to overpower and control their victims. Bullying usually begins when the victim reacts in a frightened or passive way to the bullying.

When fourth grader Caesar was called a "faggot" by a group of boys during recess, his response was to blush, something he couldn't stop from happening. That did it for the bullies, and for the rest of the year they made his life miserable with taunts and jeers, waiting for him to blush.

Sixth grader Kerry is overweight and is regularly teased by a group of popular girls on the bus who go after her about being too fat to fit into the seat. Kerry tries to hold back her tears, but they roll down her face, and the girls ridicule her for crying.

The common characteristics of children who are bullied are:

- They are considered "different" or do not "fit in" in a conventional way in personality, clothes, interests, or physical looks.
- They are seen as physically weak or have a passive personality or are sensitive.
- They are smart and get good grades.
- They are overtly emotional and may cry, stammer, or blush.
- They are overweight.
- They are members of racial/ethnic minorities.

Research indicates that children with learning, physical, or other educational needs are at a high risk of being bullied. Those with low self-esteem and poor coping skills are often easy targets. Children who are cautious, shy, or insecure are targeted by bullies because they generally respond by retreating or crying, and it is assumed by the bully that they will not react aggressively and will be easy to control. Some victims have overprotective parents, poor social and coping skills, and have not learned how to defend themselves adequately.

Listing the characteristics of victims is not in any way meant to blame the victim. They indicate what research has found about bullied kids in trying to stop bullying. A child who is sensitive, is smart, has a disability, or is deemed "different" in any way has a right to be so. Bullying has to be stopped by parents and the schools. But teaching your child how to handle bullies could help to stop them, and also build your child's social skills and confidence.

Is My Child Being Bullied?

It is not uncommon for children who are being bullied to remain silent, because they believe to tell and take action would only make the situation worse. They lose trust in authority figures to keep them safe. Chronic bullying leaves victims feeling helpless and hopeless. These children feel unsafe and unprotected at school, especially if they see that bullies get away with bullying on a daily basis. The following symptoms and behaviors may mean that your child is a victim of bullying: frequent stomachaches, headaches, bed-wetting, tension/anxiety, sadness/depression, social withdrawal, acting out with anger at home or school, drop in grades, or school refusal. Your child may come home with bruises, cuts, and torn clothing. If your child is bullied, you must act immediately, because your child's emotional and intellectual growth and development will be hindered by bullying. You may want to go directly to the bully's parents, but that might not be best unless you know something about them—parents of bullies may get defensive and make matters worse. Talk to the school to determine the best course of action.

✎ Guidelines for Helping Your Child Deal with Bullies

Talk to your child openly about bullying and teach her how to defend herself in positive ways that will lessen or stop the bullying, but only if she feels safe and help is at hand.

1. Stay calm and talk to your child about what is happening, promising to listen to her ideas about what to do about the situation. Tell her that bullying is not acceptable in any form.
2. Determine quickly if your intervention is needed or you can wait until she has first tried to work things out.
3. Teach your child to be confident: to put her head up, shoulders back, and walk away; to speak up and say, "No!" or "Stop saying that about me!" with confidence and then walk away; or to confront the bully verbally and say, "Why do you say those things about me?"
4. Teach your child to pretend that the teasing or name-calling is not hurtful or how to shrug off the bullying and walk away, even though it does hurt. (See the Shrugging Shoulders exercise at the end of the chapter.) Or teach her to joke about it with the bully. For example, if she is teased about her clothes, tell her to say something like, "Yep, I got dressed without

the lights on this morning" and then immediately leave the scene, or begin talking to another child about something else.

5. Early on, help your child learn social skills, make friends, and stick with them in school. Talk to the parents of your child's friends to teach the group how to defend each other if bullied. Bullies are less likely to bully a group, especially an assertive one.

6. Teach your child to speak out by getting help from teachers if she is bullied, or if she is a witness to bullying.

To encourage positive coping skills and strategies in your child, model assertive behavior; accept people for their differences; and be kind, compassionate, and empathic. Encourage your child to make friends near home and to engage in activities and interests that make her feel good about herself. Ask if she would like to learn martial arts to build confidence. Monitor your child's computer and cell phone use to check for cyber-bullying; your child may be a victim or perpetrator. Tell your child that even if she is being bullied, she cannot become a bully, but that together and with the school's help solutions will be found to the problem.

What Can Schools Do?

Schools have to identify the problem and come up with a no-bullying, nonviolence policy that states that any type of bullying is unacceptable and will be dealt with by the school administration. The policy has to be clearly defined and taught to staff, parents, and students. Effective antibullying programs include educating school personnel, students, and parents about bullying and its effect on the individual and the school environment; peer counseling; enacting "speak up about bullying" programs for children, and telling them exactly what to do and who to go to if they are bullied or witness bullying; involving parent organizations to get parents active in the school, and to get to know each other and each other's children; teaching about tolerance and diversity; and promoting group activities or cooperative learning, where children can get to know each other.

Overcoming Bullying Clinic

Because victims of bullying generally react in an overt way to the harassment, it will be important to teach your child how to calm herself quickly and feel centered, so she can think clearly about what to do, keep symptoms of anxiety from showing, and build confidence about being able to control herself instead of feeling under the control of the bully. The prerequisites are breathing (Chapter 14), staying in the moment (Chapter 15), and facing fear and letting go (Chapter 16).

ROLE-PLAY WITH THE BULLY IN FANTASY

First, read the exercises in Chapter 16 to learn how to set up guided imagery for your child. With your child, write down exactly what happens when he is bullied.

WALKING TALL AND SAYING "NO!" WITH CONFIDENCE

First, have your child calm herself with breathing while sitting in a chair or lying down for a few minutes. Next, have her imagine herself walking in school with her shoulders back and her head held high feeling confident that she can handle the bully situation—and she can. Have her picture that when the bullying starts, she says, "No, stop that!" in a confident tone. Then she moves away from the bully. Time for two minutes, have her rest, then imagine the same thing again. Repeat five to ten times more. Ask her if she feels more confident after she imagines that she is. Now, have her play that part while looking at herself in a full-length mirror. Have her practice until she feels that her tone and body language will tell the bully that she is not a victim anymore. Say to her that she is only to do this if she feels safe and that help is at hand. If she cannot follow through with this exercise at school with the real bully, have her practice more, or move on to another exercise.

SHRUGGING SHOULDERS: I DON'T CARE!

Teach your child that when name-calling or taunting begins she will "shrug" her shoulders in a nonchalant manner, as if she doesn't care and the bullying is not important. Also have her add a little smile, and then walk away from the bully. Practice in the same way you did in the Walking Tall exercise.

ROLE-PLAY WITH THE BULLY

After your child has mastered the previous exercises, role-play what she is going to do with you or an older child playing the bully. As you practice, keep changing the bully's response to your child's newfound confidence and reaction, so you can problem solve with your child about what might happen and prepare her for surprises.

PREPARING A PLAN OF ACTION

With your child, prepare a plan if she is bullied: what to do first, what exercises she will use, when she should seek help and safety, who she should notify, what she should say when reporting bullying for herself or others.

☙

Bullies are found in every school all over the world. And it is likely your child will be meeting up with bullies throughout her life. Teach her the skills that will "bullyproof" her: good social skills and the ability to connect with others, feeling self-worth, assertiveness, confidence, and having the courage to speak up for herself and others. Remember that children are not able to defend themselves in certain situations, and that for her own safety you will have to intervene even if your child wishes you to stay out of it.

CHAPTER 12

Parental and Family Conflict and Issues

☙

W
HEN CHILDREN FACE MAJOR CHANGES, SUCH AS MOVING TO a new house and school, or losses, such as divorce, family conflict, or trauma due to domestic violence or having addicted parents, they become frightened, feel unstable and unsafe, and are at high risk of developing chronic anxiety or other mental conditions. These stressed children often play out family problems in the classroom by having difficulty in doing homework and taking tests, getting poor grades, having behavior problems, and withdrawing from social activity. Children who are already struggling in school with learning disabilities, or behavioral and social issues, will likely have an exacerbation of their problems when their home life is unsettled or troubled.

Ellen, in second grade, liked school and had good grades and lots of friends. She moved to a new house and school midyear. Although originally excited about the move, when it came time to leave she was sad and became angry at her parents. Ellen's adjustment to the new school has been difficult because she is having trouble connecting with the girls in her class. Also, the curriculum is harder and Ellen's grades are not as good as they were in her other school. Now every morning Ellen cries to stay home, and her parents are worried.

Denzel, a sixth grader, originally hated school in kindergarten and first grade. He was diagnosed with dyslexia at the end of first grade, and with special classes, tutoring, his parents' help, and his own hard work became a good student. He was actually looking forward to middle school and had plans to get involved in sports for the first time. But this year, his father was shipped out to Iraq and killed. Devastated, Denzel lost all interest in school. He refuses to go to school because he fears something will happen to his mother when he is away from home. When she tries to get him out of the house to catch the bus, he lashes out angrily, and recently threw one of his schoolbooks at her. Denzel also recently hit a kid in class who was bothering him and was sent to the principal's office.

Harry is in fourth grade and suffers from generalized anxiety. He can't concentrate in class, feels sick before taking a test and tests poorly, and almost never does his homework. Harry is in jeopardy of failing the grade and being left back. He has a few friends in school but generally keeps to himself. His mother tries to keep him on track, but home is chaotic. His father is an alcoholic and regularly flies into rages when he is drunk. He has hit Harry's mother in front of Harry and often yells at Harry and his younger sister for no reason. Harry is terrified that his mother will get seriously hurt or that his father will hurt him or his sister. He lives in a minefield, never knowing when an explosion is going to go off.

Crystal, who is in fifth grade, has poor grades and frequent absences. She suffers from migraines and has trouble sleeping. Unbeknownst to the school, Crystal's father is an alcoholic and also smokes marijuana regularly. Although he maintains a regular job, when he drinks he becomes verbally abusive toward Crystal's mother, and recently pushed her around the kitchen when she confronted him about being drunk. Her mother is depressed and spends a good deal of time watching TV, leaving Crystal to take on the role of housewife and mother to her younger brother. When Crystal's teacher or guidance counselor attempts to find out what is wrong, Crystal stonewalls them, and her mother has had only one *meeting with the school, saying that Crystal's migraines are the problem.*

Any major life change or ongoing conflict at home leaves children vulnerable to anxiety and other emotional problems. For some children, school is the only stable environment in their lives. It becomes a daily place to go to and forget about their troubles, where they are accepted by friends, and are positively reinforced for their efforts and behavior by adults. However, for other children who are struggling to cope with problems at home, school becomes another source of stress and anxiety.

It is important for parents to alert the school of any problems at home, so steps can be taken to help the child stay on track in school, and even find comfort there, such as by talking to the guidance counselor or getting extra time for taking tests. In this chapter, we will discuss some of the common parental and family issues that cause school anxiety, along with guidelines that will help parents or other caring adults aid children to navigate these difficult life situations.

Moving to a New Home or School

Moving to a new home and entering a new school can be both an exciting and a nerve-wracking experience for a child. It may be fun packing and thinking about a new room, new friends, new school, but leaving behind the familiar and facing the unknown usually causes some anxiety. The questions about the new school that worry a child will likely include, "What if I don't make friends?" or "What if I don't like the teacher?" or "What if the work is harder?" The unknowns about change are what create anxiety, although the child's personality and how he or she handles life situations will be a factor in how the child adjusts to the change. The following guidelines can help your child make the transition to a new school as smoothly as possible:

1. Talk to your child about the move as soon as you know it will take place. Listen to his concerns, feelings of loss, or

anger about the change without judgment. For example, if your child says, "I'm worried I won't make new friends," don't say, "That's silly. There is nothing to worry about." He is worried, change is hard, so just listen and comfort him and together decide on proactive activities for making friends. Tell him his feelings are normal under the circumstances.

2. Learn how to calm yourself and to roll with the punches. Teach this outlook to your child and other family members—the calmer everyone is, the smoother the move and adjustment will be.

3. Leave adequate time for him to say good-bye to neighbors and classmates.

4. If the new school is within driving distance, take a trip to it before he begins. Familiarize him with the building and classroom, have him meet his teacher, and discuss the curriculum with him.

5. If the move is far away, go online to the school's website with him.

6. Be patient with your child. Expect an adjustment period that could take a few months to a year. Try to keep daily routines as normal as possible.

To help your child socially, as soon you can, get yourself and your family linked to organizations like PTA/PTO, scouts, or religious-affiliated youth groups. Attend neighborhood parties. If your child was involved in activities outside of school, such as martial arts or dance class, try to get her to sign up as soon as possible. Sometimes moves are forced due to divorce or other family problems. If so, and your child is not adjusting well, seek professional help.

There's a New Baby in the House

The majority of children who have to make way for a sibling have feelings, for a while at least, that they are being replaced, and that does not feel good. Common reactions or behaviors are regression or acting like a baby, which includes wetting the bed or pants, wanting a bottle, thumb sucking, and not wanting to leave mommy or go to school or do schoolwork. Older children may begin to act out aggressively at parents, the new baby, or in school. These behaviors include throwing tantrums, biting, hitting, kicking, yelling, refusing to go to school, or being disruptive in class. The following guidelines can help your child adjust to a new sibling:

1. Tell your child about the new baby, listen to his feelings, and continue to assure him that he is loved and special to you.
2. Include him in the preparations for the baby's arrival. Tell him what changes will take place with a baby in the house: Babies need lots of attention; they cry; the baby won't be able to play with him for a long time. If you know someone with a new baby, find out if he can visit them.
3. Find age-appropriate books about bringing a new baby home to read to him.
4. Make special time for your child after the baby is born, and listen to how he feels about the changes.
5. If your child regresses, don't make a big deal about it. Allow it rather than punish the behavior; it's normal and will pass. If aggression arises, tell your child the baby is not to be harmed. Hitting a baby is not allowed. Do acknowledge his anger and teach him acceptable ways to express it such as writing about it, working through it with art materials, or going outside and yelling his anger out at the sky.

When you come home with the baby, have someone else carry it so you can go to your older child immediately. Tell family members and friends to pay attention to him, too, when they visit, and have special things for him when people show up with baby gifts. Allow your older child to participate in baby care, for example, helping the baby get dressed or pushing the stroller. Make sure your older child keeps up with his routine, friends, and activities in school and at home.

Fighting, Arguing, and Domestic Violence

Children who have to listen to their parents' constant arguing and fighting get worried, scared, and anxious. It is not uncommon for these children to have problems at school because of the conflict at home. What they have to listen to is parents yelling at each other, name-calling, taunts, and threats of divorce, all common in nasty parental fighting. If the arguing takes a physical turn, then the child is a prisoner of domestic violence and either witnesses it or becomes a recipient of it. Children in a conflict-ridden family often believe the fighting is their fault. They have trouble concentrating in school and do poorly. They bury feelings about what is happening and develop anxiety disorders, depression, and other emotional problems, and they act out aggressively at home and school. What children require from parents is consistent love, kindness, security, safety, and direction. Chronic arguing and domestic violence are traumatic for children. The following guidelines can help your child:

1. Do an honest assessment of your family dynamics. Involve your partner or spouse if possible. Take steps to make changes. If there is violence, get professional help immediately for the whole family. Or, if necessary, prepare to go to a safe place with family or friends, or go to a shelter.
2. Take a long, hard look at whether your behavior is hurting your child. You have the power to change your home environment so that everyone in it will thrive.
3. Learn to control emotions, to talk instead of fight, to deal with conflict in a positive adult manner. Model these behaviors to your child.

Watch your child for signs of stress, unhappiness, and anxiety. Reassure your child that mommy and daddy are arguing, but it is not his fault. Allow him to express himself. Try to spend time alone with your child doing fun things, and if possible, learn how to have quality family time.

Divorce

Children whose parents divorce face a trying time. The world as they know it is ending and a new way of life is unfolding, which could include parental fighting, a custody battle, changes in financial lifestyle, stepparents and their children, moving to a new home, not being able to see the noncustodial parent as much as the child would like, or losing contact with that parent completely. Divorce can mean a change in the whole fabric of the child's life, and adjusting to that can be extremely difficult. How well a child adjusts to divorce very much depends on how parents react and respond to each other and their children. If you are going through a divorce, remember that parenting skills often decrease due to the emotional upheaval, so pay extra attention to your child's feelings and responses.

Children of divorce often experience symptoms such as sadness/grief; fear; anxiety; anger/aggression; acting-out behaviors; sleeping and eating problems; and anxiety, behavioral, and academic problems in school. The following guidelines can help your child cope with divorce:

1. Along with your spouse, talk to your child about the divorce, assuring him that he is loved and will be protected by both of you. Tell him what will have to change and what routines will remain the same. The less you have to change initially, the better.

2. No matter how you feel about your ex, keep conflict private and to a minimum, and make custody agreements fair and flexible. The more a child can see both parents, the better the outcome for the child.

3. Do not put your child in the middle of the divorce—he is not a pawn.

4. Tell the school what is happening to alert his teacher to watch him for potential problems, as well as be a caring adult figure in his life at this trying time.

5. Try to have a large network of adult support for your child:

grandparents, other family members, and friends. Also, keep your child's social contacts up by arranging for playdates.

6. Engage your child in positive experiences. For example, if you have to move, have your child help with decorating his room, like picking out paint colors and posters to hang. Maybe your child is interested in joining a club or group, such as scouts or chorus; learning a new activity, such as dance or karate; or taking up a hobby.

Allow your child to express his feelings freely without judging him or trying to make him feel better—let him talk; you listen. Acting-out behaviors must be addressed, but be sure to tell your child that you love him, that it's his behavior you disapprove of. Find reading material on helping your child handle divorce. Although it may be difficult to do, try to work with your ex-spouse to ease the stress of divorce on your child.

Parent's Illness

When a parent becomes ill, the household is thrown into a crisis, changing family dynamics and the roles of family members. At this difficult time, when children are trying to cope with and make sense of what is occurring, they will need comfort and understanding from adults who are important to them.

Children with an ill parent often fear the death of the parent and worry about what will happen to them in the future. A parent may be away in the hospital for long stays or at home but unable to interact with the child adequately because of disease, leading to feelings of being abandoned. The illness may change the parent's physical appearance, making the child afraid or ashamed and guilty about feeling that way. Anger is commonly directed at the sick parent for abandoning the child, causing the child to feel guilty.

Children may also believe that somehow they are the cause of the illness because they were bad, angry, or didn't do what they were supposed to. Schoolwork often suffers because worrying about a sick parent interferes with concentration. Social activity may decrease because of depression or because seeing a friend's healthy parent is a painful reminder of what the child doesn't have anymore. To help children cope with a sick parent use the following guidelines:

1. Talk to the child at an age-appropriate level about what is happening. Listen to the child's feelings and mention other things she might be feeling, and that it is normal.
2. Assemble a team of adults who can support, listen to, and comfort the child. Include family, teachers and school staff, and clergy. Get professional help as needed.
3. As the parent who is well, find support and respite to help you cope and to allow you to spend time alone with your children.
4. Keep the child's routine as normal as possible, and team with the school to help your child get needed extra time to stay focused and up-to-date with schoolwork.

Death of a Parent

When a parent dies, the surviving parent generally has a tough time helping a child cope with the death as the parent also deals with the loss. It's important to explain the death to the child in clear terms, and your child's age will determine how you approach this. A kindergarten child who may not be able to grasp the fact that the parent's death is a permanent loss might question over and over, "When is Mommy coming home?" Be patient and explain to the child in simple terms what happened; for example, she got hurt or was sick, but she will not be back.

Between ages six and seven, children begin to understand that death is final, but they often think that the parent will "magically" return if they are good, or they could become frightened of death personified by scary media images. If this occurs, simply explain what death means. Make decisions about a child attending a parent's funeral depending on the child's age and emotional state. Have a caretaker for the child at the funeral if she does attend.

Grief is a long process and children experience it differently than adults. They may have no outward reaction, or they may withdraw, be anxious and hyper, get angry or scared, regress to babyhood, act out, have nightmares, not want to go to school, or lose interest in playing with friends. Whatever the reaction, be patient, comforting, and seek professional help if grief symptoms worsen or persist. The following guidelines can help your child:

1. Openly talk to your child about the death, and listen to your child's feelings.
2. Explain what will happen to the body, what a funeral is, where the parent's body will be taken.
3. Alert the school and ask for support for your child while she is in school. Ask the guidance counselor to call your child in periodically to check on her. Grades may drop, and interests and friendships may cease, but be patient and understanding.

Be sure to find as much support as you can for yourself, your child, and family members by reaching out to family, friends, and organizations for help at this difficult time. Assure your child that she will always be cared for and safe even though this occurred.

Addicted Parents

Children who live with a parent addicted to drugs or alcohol often live in chaotic and abusive homes, where they may be the recipient of or witness to verbal, physical, or sexual abuse. The resulting cost to the child is trauma. Some addicted parents function well within the norms of society. They go to work regularly, clean the house, and seemingly take care of their children. In some homes, no verbal or physical abuse takes place and the addiction is well hidden.

Whatever way addiction manifests itself, it takes a heavy toll on children, who often take on the adult roles and become "little adults" and the "peacemaker," trying to calm parents and keep the household running; blunt themselves emotionally; or act out at home and school.

The short- and long-term problems these children face include chronic anxiety, depression, and other emotional problems; a high risk of becoming addicted or developing a serious mental illness; physical complaints, such as chronic stomach and head pain; or, due to high stress, weakened immune systems, which could eventually lead to disease. They may also be at risk of having learning and behavior problems. Children of an addicted parent also feel alone, unloved, and unlovable, and learn not to trust anyone or have close relationships for fear of being betrayed and hurt.

✎ Guidelines for Helping Children of an Addicted Parent

It is crucial that children of an addicted parent be supported by caring adults, who could include a nonaddicted parent, family members, friends, teachers, guidance counselors, sports coaches, or religious leaders. The following guidelines can help:

1. Build rapport with the child. Allow him to talk and listen without judging the addicted parent. Support the child in his love for the parent, but not the addicted parent's behavior.
2. Explain addiction in age-appropriate language to the child; use educational materials, too.
3. Prepare the child in taking safety measures if he is in danger from his parent's threats or abuse.
4. Contact the school so teachers and staff understand why the child is struggling with grades, peers, and so forth. Ask how the school can help, for example, talking with the teacher, guidance counselors, or coaches.

Find a mental health professional experienced in working with children of addicted parents, look at community mental health clinics as well as private practitioners. Family counseling and area support groups are other important sources not only for child therapy but for information on finding a professional who could set up an intervention for the addicted parent.

෧෨

Major life changes are difficult to adjust to and children who are faced with change, such as moving to a new school, need parental or adult care, support, and patience, as they come to terms with the new life while giving up the old one. With time, most children will adapt to change and become successful at home and at school. A child who faces daily conflict at home is vulnerable to mental health problems and school failure. It may require a community of adults consisting of parents, teachers, counselors, or law-enforcement personnel to intervene at home and school to give aid and support in the best interests of the child.

CHAPTER 13

My Child Has Learning, Physical, or Emotional Challenges

߷

C HILDREN WITH MEDICAL, PHYSICAL, OR EMOTIONAL DISABILI-
ties have the same needs and desires as any other student for
adjusting to and trying to succeed in school. They want to learn
the class work, do well on tests, get good grades, and make friends. But
students with disabilities have greater struggles and are at a higher risk
of school anxiety because of feeling different and needing to overcome
that bias, being unable to keep up in class, not having adequate classroom accommodations for success, and being stigmatized and often
teased about being "stupid," "weird," or "ugly." These students attempt
to fit into the school culture, which mirrors the greater one that emphasizes success, high achievement, physical beauty, and popularity.
This chapter discusses the common physical, learning, and emotional
disabilities that are generally seen in regular classrooms. Guidelines and
exercises are included to enable you to help your child navigate the
learning environment. For more information, see the resources section
at the end of the book.

What Is Inclusion?

In 1973, Congress passed the Individuals with Disabilities Education
Act (IDEA), with the goal of accommodating special-needs students
so they could be taught in regular classrooms instead of going to special
schools or attend special classes along with regular ones. The Education for All Handicapped Children Act was passed in 1975, giving

every child the right to a public education in the least restrictive environment possible. These acts were modified, and in 1991 the federal government defined thirteen categories of disabilities: autism, deaf-blindness, deafness, hearing impairment, mental retardation, multiple disabilities, orthopedic impairment, other health impairment, serious emotional disturbance, special learning disability, speech or language impairment, traumatic brain injury, and visual impairment.

Along with these changes, educators implemented a tool-and-team approach to determine the best environment for the special-education student called an individual education plan (IEP). An IEP asks a series of questions to find out if a student can succeed in a regular classroom if given supplementary aids and services. Some questions are: Will a regular classroom benefit the student? What accommodations are needed for the student to succeed? How will the student's disability affect other students academically and emotionally? Will the student's special needs take up too much of the teacher's time?

Changes and adjustments to inclusion are ongoing as schools grapple with the unique problems of special-needs students, which include coming up with a fair system of accountability that applies to all students, the types of high school diplomas awarded to these students, the dropout rate of 29.4 percent according to the federal government's Department of Special Education and Rehabilitation, and the lack of research.

There are many students who struggle socially and academically who fall outside the criteria for special needs because they cannot be formally diagnosed. These children may be labeled lazy or defiant, but many have mild to moderate degrees of conditions like learning disorders or ADHD, anxiety, depression, or other unobservable causes of their problems. It will take awareness, sensitivity, and good detective work on the part of parents and teachers to find solutions to help these students.

It's Hard Being Different

From infancy on, children form a good part of their identity based on how others respond to them, and vice versa. Children who have physical, mental, or emotional disabilities learn at some point in their young lives that they are considered negatively "different" by adults and peers, which is magnified when they leave the safety of their home and enter school.

Each child with a disability has a unique experience due to his or her personality, innate coping mechanisms, family, school, social support, and type of disability he or she lives with. In the next section, we'll take a look at the different challenges these children face, and how parents and the school can help.

Being "Different" in School

Children who have physical impairments may be wheelchair bound, deformed, or not able to speak clearly. Children with learning disabilities struggle daily because they are often unable to keep up in class. Emotional problems make some children lose control of their behavior, turning off peers, frustrating teachers, or making concentration on a test impossible. Children with any of these problems are likely to experience anxiety symptoms that can make the school experience a nightmare and result in anxiety disorders, depression, or long-term negative attitudes and beliefs about self. Bullying and isolation by peers makes the school day even less bearable.

Decades of research indicates that disabled students have a greater chance of being negatively viewed by school personnel and nondisabled students. Children with disabilities may be pulled out of their school and sent to a special school, losing a familiar structure and friendships. They may also be less likely to be seen as college material at home and at school and not have the same academic opportunities as nondisabled students, or develop the self-image of not being smart and capable although their intellectual capabilities are either the same as or above those of nondisabled children. Parental, family, and school support and guidance can go a long way in helping disabled children adjust to school, succeed academically and socially, and discover their strengths so they can have the best school experience possible and reach their potential.

What Are Learning Disabilities?

A learning disability is a disorder in one or more mental processes that can affect the ability to read, write, spell, listen, think, or understand and do math. It is not a reflection of your child's real intelligence or potential because most children with learning difficulties have average to above-average intelligence. Learning disabilities occur because of the way the brain receives and processes information. With support and guidance, a learning-disabled child can be taught how to unlock his unique way of learning and become a successful student. Learning problems may be caused by mental or intellectual handicaps, attention problems, visual or auditory conditions, physical illnesses, emotional or behavioral health, family problems, and school worries such as being bullied.

The U.S. Government estimates that about 10 percent of school-age children have a learning problem that includes one of the following:

- *Dyslexia*—difficulty in being accurate and/or fluent in recognizing words, spelling, and the relationship between letter sounds necessary to identify words
- *Dysgraphia*—problems with spelling, handwriting, and putting thoughts and ideas down in writing
- *Dyscalculia*—the inability to understand, hear, and write numbers and learn math concepts
- *ADHD*—not a learning disorder but often causes children to have problems learning because they are easily distracted, can't sit still in class, and have trouble concentrating

Christy, a second grader who struggles with reading, writing, and math, was diagnosed with both dyslexia and dyscalculia. She attends special classes for those subjects and spends the rest of the time in her regular classroom. Christy struggles to keep up with the work and often feels overwhelmed. She feels stigmatized in school and different from her classmates, who sometimes tease her about going to the "dumb class." Christy is slowly learning to understand her disability, to appreciate her strengths, and is learning to say to classmates, "I'm smart too. I just learn differently."

What Are the Signs of a Learning Difficulty?

Learning problems likely become apparent when a child enters school. If your child exhibits any of the following persistent problems or behaviors, contact the school immediately: has slow vocabulary development; has difficulty pronouncing words, learning numbers or shapes, or remembering class work such as times tables; has poor handwriting; has difficulty copying work; has speech and language problems; won't read out loud; has poor concentration or is restless, easily frustrated, or impulsive; shuts down when the work is too hard; often forgets homework; has trouble making friends; or is anxious, depressed, and refuses to go to school.

Physical Conditions and Disabilities

Physical disabilities are any conditions that prevent or restrict body movement or control of body movement. However, children with numerous physical disabilities can still participate in regular classrooms. Physical disabilities include:

- *Muscular Dystrophy*—causes weakening of muscle fibers
- *Spina Bifida*—spinal cord does not develop normally in utero
- *Cerebral Palsy*—damage to parts of the brain that control movement

Some children have acquired brain and spinal injuries, which are conditions due to birth or accidents. Others have multiple disabilities that include physical conditions and other disabilities such as intellectual, visual, or hearing impairments; speech difficulties such as stuttering; and medical conditions such as asthma, seizure disorders, or epilepsy.

Estefan is a sixth grader who was diagnosed with muscular dystrophy (MD) at age four. Kindergarten and first grade were successful for him, but by second grade the disease's symptoms were becoming more pronounced, such as frequently falling down, having difficulty getting up when he is sitting, being able to walk only on his toes in a kind of waddle, and being easily fatigued after physical activity. Little by little, classmates began to avoid him. Some even teased him when he fell or about how he walked. Playing with friends after school became almost impossible because of his physical limitations. He used to beg his parents to let him stay home on school mornings, and he suffered from test anxiety. Eventually, he came to a degree of acceptance about his condition, and now he studies hard, is a top student, and pursues many interests. Now in a wheelchair, Estefan is still mostly isolated from classmates, but he has made a few good friends in the school's science club and near his home.

Children with physical disabilities may have average or above-average intelligence, but they have to cope with the restrictions that these conditions place on them such as being wheelchair bound, deformed, unable to control body movement, bladder and/or bowel problems, or seizures. Long leaves of absence for treatments or hospitalizations will mean pressure in having to keep up with schoolwork. Trying to connect with peers can be very difficult under these circumstances and anxiety, depression, social isolation, and low self-esteem are common. It is not uncommon for classmates and even school personnel to mistakenly believe that these children are not intelligent, capable, and creative.

Emotional Disturbances

Children with emotional disturbances exhibit persistent behaviors that over time negatively affect academic performance. These include having trouble learning although no physical cause is present; being immature for their age; having tantrums or crying fits; or having poor coping skills or behavioral problems. The child can exhibit aggressive behavior toward self and others or can be hyperactive and impulsive with a short attention span. Others have difficulty forming and maintaining suitable interpersonal relationships with peers or teachers or have pervasive sadness, depression, and anxiety. Emotional disturbances include the following:

- Anxiety disorders: generalized anxiety disorder, obsessive-compulsive disorder, panic disorder, posttraumatic stress disorder, social anxiety disorder, or phobias
- Depression: severe depression or bipolar disorder
- Schizophrenia

Chanise, a third grader, has been treated for separation anxiety disorder, generalized anxiety disorder, and depression since kindergarten. She is very sensitive to how other children respond to her, and often thinks they are talking about her or that they don't like her. When she takes a test, she often cries. School is generally difficult for her. Chanise still has trouble leaving home for school, and rarely accepts invitations to play at a friend's home or to go to parties. She would rather stay home than play with friends. When she is away from home, she feels sad about not being with her family and will often start crying. Chanise spends part of her school day in an emotional support class, and gets help in the resource room with reading.

Many children who are neurotic or maladjusted do not meet the IDEA criteria for special educational services, but they need help just the same. If your child falls into this category, seek help from the school and a mental health specialist.

Autism Spectrum Disorders

Autism is a brain disorder that affects the development of a child's ability to communicate, socially interact with others, and interact and adapt to his environment. Autism is diagnosed along a continuum from mild to severe. Several types of autism have been defined. Classic autism (autistic disorder) is the most severe of autistic disorders, with pervasive impairments such as flat affect and rigid routine. Asperger's disorder is severe impairment in social interaction, with the individual exhibiting restricted outside interests and repetitive behaviors, but does not have the profound impairments in classic autism. Rett syndrome is a neurological degenerative disorder that reduces muscle tone and leads to multiple disabilities and dependent care. Pervasive developmental disorder (PDD) is diagnosed when there is severe impairment in social, verbal, and nonverbal communication. Symptoms vary from those of classic autism and onset is later in age.

Chronic Medical Conditions

Children with chronic illness face a risk of anxiety because they may often be absent from class when ill or for treatments or long hospital stays, making it hard for them to keep up with schoolwork. They often feel different and isolated from their peers. Common childhood chronic illnesses include cancer, cystic fibrosis, diabetes, epilepsy, and asthma.

Coping with Your Child's Disability

A child's disability also affects parents and family members. If your child was born with an obvious disability or became disabled through an accident or disease, or you discovered he has trouble learning, you probably went through a grief process. Maybe you felt guilty thinking you could have done something to change things, or angry that this happened to your child. You may worry about your child growing up and being able to lead an independent life. Siblings may feel angry and resentful that they are not getting enough attention from parents, or they may be ashamed of their sibling's disability. It is important that you take action and seek help from the school and other professionals for the welfare of your child and family members.

How Can I Help My Disabled Child?

Success in school comes from a combination of many factors and parental support and guidance is at the top of the list. Whether your child has been diagnosed with a mental, physical, or emotional condition that makes her eligible for an IEP or not, there are many ways you can help your child:

- Develop stress management skills yourself by learning how to relax and stay calm under pressure. This will enable you to make good decisions for your child and to communicate effectively with your child, the school, and family members. Also, modeling how to cope well with adversity is a powerful lesson for your child.
- Do not yell at or demean your child even though you feel frustrated or angry because of your child's limitations, emotions, or behaviors, because doing so will only make things worse. Learn how to handle the stress. Do not allow family, friends, or others to tease or put down your child, no matter who they are.
- Teach your child how to de-stress and relax in and out of school with the exercises and suggestions contained in this book.
- Educate yourself about your child's disability and come prepared for school meetings. Be a good listener, advocate for your child intelligently and assertively, offer suggestions to school personnel on how to socially integrate your child, and talk about academics. If you are unhappy with school policy, become involved and organize with other parents to make positive changes for all children.
- Have open discussions with your child about his disability without labeling him. Talk about "limitations" and "strengths" and that we all have them. Allow your child to discuss his feelings and problems due to his disability. Be an active listener.
- Encourage your child to participate in problem solving when things aren't going well. Don't jump in to rescue him. Learning to make choices to work out problems, even though failure is an option, is empowering and builds self-confidence.

Talk about what "we can do as a team," and how to handle failure.

- Praise your child's effort, not just the end result—make effort count!
- Help your child to explore other strengths and talents outside of school, such as having a good personality; being kind; loving animals; engaging in creative activities, sports, or hobbies; or participating in social organizations.
- Help your child create a special place at home to do schoolwork, at-home reading, and other creative activities. Be involved with schoolwork, but not overbearing. Teach independence.
- Teach your child to be a proactive learner. School worksheets are a passive form of learning, as are watching TV and even playing on the computer. Turn them off and engage your child in activities such as food shopping, cooking, cleaning, gardening, pet care, looking at the stars, and hiking.

What the School Can Do

Schools are required to meet the criteria of IDEA, but policies vary by school district. Before you register your child, explore all the educational options available in your area. Meet with teachers and support staff and use the following questions as a guideline:

- Are teachers and staff trained to work with my child's particular problem or condition, for example, allowing extra time on tests, using a spellchecker or calculator, or taking an exam orally?
- Can the school meet my child's technical needs, such as ramps, teacher microphones, and computer-assisted technology, so he will feel he's on a level playing field with other students?
- Does the school create an in-school team of teachers, counselors, psychologists, nurses, and administrators for a comprehensive approach to children with disabilities?

- How will the teacher help my child build relationships with other school personnel and classmates?
- Does the school foster a positive approach to building children's confidence by recognizing each student's unique qualities and talents?
- Does the school promote and educate students and staff on diversity and have a strong policy against bullying?

Exercises

There are many exercises throughout this book that will benefit your child. If your child is able to learn the breathing, staying-in-the-moment, and float and loosen techniques, teach her those. Set up a classroom for mock practice in test taking and participating in class. Use role-play to help your child approach and interact with classmates and teachers. Read the exercises at the end of Chapters 4, 5, and 6, and adapt them to your child's problem and condition. The following is a fun exercise for you to do with your child.

CREATING AN "ABILITY" ALBUM

Tell your child that together you are going to create an album of people who achieved their goals and dreams, even though they had the same condition or disability as your child does. Buy a photo album or scrapbook. On the first page have your child paste his favorite photograph of himself. Leave room for an autobiography for a later time. Go online and search for famous people who overcame disabilities. Whoopi Goldberg, actress; Jewel, pop singer; George Patton, military general; Edward Hallowell, physician; Walt Disney, cartoonist and founder of Disneyland; and Thomas Edison, inventor, all have or had learning disabilities. Franklin Roosevelt, the thirty-second president of the United States; Helen Keller, author; and Stephen Hawking, physicist, had physical conditions. Mike Wallace, journalist, and Patty Duke, actress, have mood disorders, as did author Kurt Vonnegut.

Next, find a photograph of the person or persons if possible and paste it on a page leaving room for biographies. If the people are still alive, and you can't find pictures, try to find their addresses and help your child write a letter explaining the exercise and requesting a photograph and maybe an autograph too. Have your child research each person's life and write the biography, and help him as needed. Discuss the person's life and struggles with your child. Ask him why he thinks the person succeeded in spite of the disability. Ask your child what he thinks he has to do to overcome the limitations of his condition. After your child has finished filling at least half the album, ask him to write his autobiography whenever he feels ready.

Having a child diagnosed with a disability is a tough road to travel, requiring lots of energy and focus on helping the child. However, you and your family need assistance in processing the emotional fallout. Find someone who is trustworthy and a good listener with whom to talk. Learn how to manage stress and time, have realistic expectations of your child and yourself, get professional help, and create a solid support system for yourself and your family.

CHAPTER 14

Learn to Breathe to Feel at Ease

As you read through this book, you'll notice that in every Overcoming School Anxiety Clinic, learning how to breathe correctly is a prerequisite. Diaphragmatic breathing, or belly breathing, is the key to overcoming school anxiety no matter what the reason: test anxiety, learning problems, bullying, or low self-esteem. Yes, just learning a type of breathing can change your child from a nervous wreck into a confident child.

Kindergartner Jamal used to scream every school morning for the first three months of school, hanging on to his mother's leg when she tried to get him to leave the house to catch the school bus. Trying to reassure him that he would be fine and have fun had no effect. By explaining to Jamal what was making him feel so frightened, and that belly breathing could help, Jamal was able to change. He learned to belly breathe, and going to school is getting easier by the day.

Belinda, in second grade, has a learning disability in math and began to have anxiety in first grade. It started when she fell behind in arithmetic because she could not understand the concepts. Panic attacks would occur when she was called to the board to solve a problem, couldn't do it, and the class would laugh. Soon she was having attacks whenever she was called on, not just during math, and could barely answer questions she knew the answer to, because she felt stupid. By learning belly breathing, and being placed in a special math class, Belinda is building her confidence and participating in class.

Before you can sell belly breathing to your child, you have to learn it yourself. The information in this chapter tells you why certain types of breathing patterns are important, how to do them, how to teach them to your child, and how to use breathing to overcome school anxiety.

What Is Belly Breathing (Diaphragmatic Breathing)?

Breathing is just breathing, right? No, wrong! Although you breathe whether you think about it or not—it is an involuntary function—breathing is also a voluntary activity. You can consciously change your breathing pattern by using different muscles and techniques to control intake and to deepen, smooth, and lengthen it. The two basic types of breathing patterns are chest breathing, associated with physical activity and the stress reaction, and diaphragmatic breathing, which is linked to reducing anxiety and becoming calm, cool, and collected.

Diaphragmatic breathing, based on yoga principles, has been used for thousands of years to link, balance, and heal mind and body. Research at major medical centers, such as Harvard and Johns Hopkins, have shown that this simple method of breathing can reduce occurrences of anxiety, depression, and other mental conditions, and ease the symptoms of some physical diseases.

Benefits of Belly Breathing

Focusing on belly breathing turns off worry and anxiety because watching your breath is to live in the moment—no past, no future, no worry. Admittedly, a tall order, but very doable. It also lowers blood pressure, eases breathing conditions such as asthma, and increases concentration and focus. It feels good while you are doing it and has a calming residual effect that lasts for hours.

During stressful times, chest breathing becomes rapid and shallow, restricting oxygen intake, increasing levels of stress hormones such as adrenaline, increasing muscle tension, causing fatigue, reducing concentration, and even triggering the fight-or-flight response. In belly breathing, the diaphragm, a dome-shaped muscle that lies between the heart and lungs and separates the chest and abdomen, moves downward when we inhale and upward when we exhale. In this process, the body fills with oxygen, respiration and blood pressure are lowered to healthy levels, and the relaxation response is engaged, signaling to the brain that the danger has passed, thereby reducing stress hormone levels and stopping the physical and mental symptoms of the fight-or-flight response.

Other benefits of this powerful breathing are feeling alert and gaining the ability to use energy resulting from anxiety to become motivated and achieve goals, gain confidence, reduce sleep problems and eating problems, increase stress management skills, decrease tantrums, and increase the ability of the immune system to fight disease and to promote good health. So, how can your child use breathing techniques to stop his school anxiety? Read on.

Belly Breathing Is Easy—Having It Work When Anxiety Hits Takes Practice

Trying to relax in an anxiety-producing situation seems impossible when the fight-or-flight response kicks in, especially for children. It's scary not to understand what is happening, or to be able to stop it. You now know how belly breathing works, but in order for breathing to countermand the power of the fight-or-flight reaction, it has to be practiced, internalized into your child's emotional being so it becomes second nature. Before you teach your child how to breathe, you have to learn it yourself. Try it!

BASIC BREATHING EXERCISE

1. Sit back in your chair, feet on the floor, hands resting in your lap.
2. Breathe only through your nose. Close your eyes.

3. Slowly inhale and exhale. When you inhale your belly expands, and at the exhale it relaxes. To make sure you are breathing properly, put your hands on your lower abdomen so that your thumbs are on your belly button. As you belly breathe, your thumbs will move in and out. Smooth and lengthen the breath from head to toe.
4. Concentrate on your breath going in and out of your body.
5. Try to slow your thoughts, giving yourself in to the exercise.

When you have finished, sit for a minute and see how you feel. Do you feel calmer? That you've taken a minivacation from the daily grind? Think about how this breathing will help your child. When it's practiced and used throughout the day, this tool will allow him to take control of his anxiety. That's a confidence booster! Now let's try belly breathing. The instructions are followed by three easy-to-learn exercises. You will need a timer.

BELLY BREATHING—FOR PARENTS

1. Practice in a quiet spot at first.
2. Breathe only through your nose to regulate and cleanse the breath.
3. Keep your chest still—you are using the diaphragm to fill your lungs with air.
4. Inhale slowly (to at least a count of three) and fill your belly like a balloon. Place your hands on your belly as explained in the previous exercise to make sure you are breathing correctly.
5. Exhale slowly (to at least a count of three) and relax your belly.
6. Keep your breath slow, smooth, long, and quiet.
7. Watch each breath as it goes in and out of your body.
8. When thoughts intrude, examine them for a second, then gently release them into the universe.

Take your time learning how to belly breathe. If you have trouble at first, don't fight the breath or give up, but try to relax into each breath.

BELLY BREATHING—LYING DOWN

1. Set the timer for two to three minutes.
2. Lie on a bed or mat on the floor. If needed, place a pillow under your head.
3. Keep your arms at your sides, or place one hand on your chest and the other on your belly to ensure that you are breathing correctly.
4. Slowly inhale and feel your belly fill. Exhale slowly and relax your belly. Continue until the time is up. Then stay in this position for a few minutes and see how you feel.

BELLY BREATHING—SITTING

1. Sit in a chair, feet on the floor, shoulders back, but relaxed.
2. Set the timer for two to three minutes. Close your eyes.
3. Inhale and exhale slowly until the time is up. Take a few minutes to see how you feel.
4. Repeat this exercise but now keep your eyes open. To stay focused, find a stationary point in the room to focus on, such as a picture on the wall or a piece of furniture. Continue until the time is up.

BELLY BREATHING—STANDING/WALKING

1. Set the timer for five minutes.
2. Stand with shoulders back, but relaxed. Distribute your weight on both legs to feel balanced and centered.
3. Begin breathing and if necessary focus on a point in the room.
4. After two minutes, begin to walk slowly.

5. Increase your speed to a fast walk while maintaining the breath. When the time is up, take a few minutes to see how you feel.

Practice belly breathing throughout the day by incorporating it into your daily activities. Examples include while sitting at a desk, walking in the house/at work, shopping, standing on line in a store, cooking, or watching TV. Practice changing from sitting to standing, and walking without breaking the rhythm of the breath. Now it's time to teach your child.

Explaining Belly Breathing to Your Child

Before you begin teaching your child belly breathing, reread Chapter 2, "Anxiety Is a Mind-Body Experience," and give him the false alarm explanation. Explain to your child that a false alarm is being set off in his brain and body when he feels unsure or afraid. To show him, make your smoke detector go off and say, "See, no fire, but the smoke detector doesn't know that, so it makes noise to warn us. That's what happens to your body; your brain doesn't know that there is no fire." Then show by either fanning the air near the detector, or putting on the exhaust fan, that the noise will stop. Tell him that you are going to teach him how to be the exhaust fan and stop the false alarm that creates a racket inside of him and causes feelings of panic.

FIRST STEPS: BELLY BREATHING WARM-UP

Following are some pre-belly-breathing games to help younger children to learn the technique or for those who are reluctant to try. Older children who are having trouble learning belly breathing may benefit from these games, too. Make practice fun, with the length of time determined by your child's age and ability to concentrate. Start with a few minutes and increase time slowly as you go. Be patient and use positive statements such as, "Great job!" or "Wow, that's hard to do, but you did it!" After practice, treat your child to time spent with you, a game, a walk, or a snack.

- *Your Belly Is a Balloon.* Have a balloon or two on hand. Explain that you want your child to think of his belly as a balloon. Have your child or yourself blow up the balloon and hold the end closed. Say, "This is what happens when you breathe in—your belly blows up." Then slowly let the air out of the balloon and say, "This is what happens when you breathe out—your belly gets flat." Blow up the balloon as many times as necessary. You can also blow up the balloon while your child feels the balloon expanding. Let the air out slowly so he can feel the balloon flattening. Next, have your child lie down placing one hand on his chest, the other on his belly. Have him push his belly in and out. Say, "See that, it feels just like the balloon."
- *Balloon Puff.* Blow up a small balloon and tie the end closed. Have your child lie down. Hold the balloon right above your child's mouth and then let it go. The goal is for your child to keep the balloon up in the air by blowing on it. Tell him to be aware of what his belly does when he blows at the balloon.
- *Blowing Bubbles.* Fill a glass halfway with your child's favorite drink. Using a straw, have him blow bubbles for a few seconds being aware that his belly is contracting. Now have him drink through the straw, his belly will expand. Continue until the drink is finished.
- *Feel Mommy's/Daddy's Belly.* Demonstrate belly breathing in different positions while your child places his hand on your belly. Also, show him how still your chest is and that you are breathing through your nose.

Now let's get to the exercises. A note: As you practice with your child, be sure you are doing your belly breathing to model the technique, to set the rhythm for the breathing, and to keep yourself and the environment calm.

BELLY BREATHING—LYING DOWN

1. Set a timer for one to two minutes. Have your child lie in bed or on a couch in a quiet room. Put a pillow under her head. Sit next to her on a chair or lie down next to her.
2. Have her place one hand on her chest, the other on her belly, and close her eyes. Tell her to imagine her breath going in and out of her belly from her head to her toe. When she thinks of other things, tell her to imagine tossing her thoughts up to the sky—then to go back to thinking about her breath.
3. She will begin inhaling and exhaling slowly, feeling her hand rise and fall. Watch her belly rhythm, and as she inhales say, "When you breathe in, your belly blows up." During her exhale say, "When you breathe out your belly flattens." Ask her if she wants you to coach her; if not, be quiet. Continue until the time is up.

VARIATION: BELLY BREATHING—LYING DOWN

1. Set the timer for one to two minutes. Place a small book on your child's belly and have her keep her eyes open.
2. Tell her to slowly inhale and exhale watching the book rise and fall. When the time is up, ask her how she feels.

Try to have your child do belly breathing every night before she goes to sleep. Practice this exercise the night before tests or whenever anxiety-producing events will occur the next day. Gradually increase practice time to five to ten minutes.

BELLY BREATHING—SITTING

1. Have your child sit in a chair similar to her chair at school. Sit near her.
2. Have her keep her feet flat on the floor and her hands in her lap, or one hand on her chest and the other on her belly. Her

shoulders should be back, but relaxed, eyes closed. Set the timer for one to two minutes.

3. Tell her as she begins to inhale and exhale slowly to take the breath down to her toes.

4. Tell her when she is distracted by thoughts to toss them into the sky and refocus on her breathing. Continue until the time is up.

5. Do the same exercise with her eyes open. Have her focus on a point in the room to maintain concentration, and to practice as if she is in school. Continue until the time is up.

Belly Breathing—Standing/Walking

1. Have your child stand tall with her shoulders back, but relaxed, hands at her sides. Set the timer for two to five minutes.

2. Have her either close her eyes or focus on a point in the room.

3. Have her to begin inhaling and exhaling slowly for two minutes. Tell her to open her eyes.

4. Have her walk slowly around the room while maintaining the breath. Increase to a normal pace or a little faster. Continue for three minutes.

Practice each exercise with your child at least three times a week. Have her practice changing from one position to another while maintaining the breath until she can do it with ease. When she has practiced enough, add distractions such as people talking, while using the computer, watching TV, playing games, at dinner, and so forth. Practice outside, too, during playtime, while riding in the car or on the school bus, when visiting with friends, in restaurants, and so on. Explain that practicing with lots of noise and commotion around her will keep her focused and those nasty "nerves" away in and out of the classroom. Teach your child to integrate belly breathing into her daily life (the way you are) until it becomes second nature and a powerful tool she can use to manage stress.

GOING TO SCHOOL

Have your child do belly breathing the night before a school day. As soon as she wakes, have her stay in bed for a few minutes and belly breathe. When she gets up, have her belly breathe as she goes about her school-morning routine. Teach her that when school worries begin, she is to toss them up to the sky and stay in the present by focusing on her breathing. Tell her to continue breathing while having breakfast, getting dressed, riding or walking to school, and as she goes through the school doors. It is important that your child use belly breathing throughout the day to keep stress hormones low and the fight-or-flight response out of sight. Give her a token from home to take to school or a note on her books to act as a reminder to belly breathe. Tell her that when she touches it or sees it, she is to belly breathe. Be sure to belly breathe yourself on school days so you will remain calm when she becomes anxious about school.

STUDYING FOR A TEST

Set up a desk and chair in your home like the schoolroom. Put the study materials on the desk, and before she starts tell your child to belly breathe for a minute or two. Say to your child, "As you study you will probably think about the test, get distracted, and may get nervous. If you do, I want you to toss that thought into the sky, belly breathe until you calm down, then continue studying." Repeat this until studying is finished. If you stay in the room, sit away from your child, and have something to do, like reading.

TEST TAKING

The night before a test have your child practice belly breathing when she thinks about the test and before she goes to bed. The next morning, have her belly breathe for a few minutes before she gets up and continue belly breathing or switch to it as she gets ready for school. Tell her to belly breathe on the bus, as she walks to class, and throughout her day until test time. Tell her that just before the test starts she should belly breathe and put both arms flat on the desk to center herself. Read through Chapter 8, "My Child Has Test Anxiety," for additional information on reducing test anxiety.

BEING CALLED ON IN CLASS/GOING TO THE BLACKBOARD

Hang a blackboard in your home schoolroom. You play the teacher and have your child sit at the desk. Practice calling on her or have her go to the board to work on a problem. Tell her that as soon as she is called on, she is to exhale slowly to release the initial tension when she hears her name called, then either answer the question or get up and go to the board belly breathing all the way. Practice asking questions she stumbles on or does not have an answer for, and then rehearse how to respond while being calm.

SOCIAL FEARS

If your child has social anxiety, make a list with her of the things about socializing that bother her. Is she shy? Afraid what she says is stupid? Is she being bullied? Afraid she won't "fit in"? If possible, observe her with peers. Look at her body language and reactions and responses. Choose one problem at a time to work on. Plan with your child where and when she can use belly breathing: at recess, when she extends an invitation to a classmate to play, when she is invited to a classmate's home. Role-play with her situations that cause worry, and have her determine how to respond, and where to use belly breathing.

SLEEPING

Belly breathing is an effective method that your child can use to fall asleep or get back to sleep if he is wakeful.

1. Have your child lie in bed, hands at his sides, eyes closed.
2. Have him begin belly breathing, and if he wishes, at the same time he can repeat a calming phrase such as, "I'm sleepy," or he can count each breath until he falls asleep.

3. Tell him that if he wakes during the night he can repeat this exercise.

A variation on the sleep exercise is to teach him to relax his whole body. As he belly breathes, have him say in a quiet voice, "Head fall asleep, neck fall asleep, shoulders fall asleep, back fall asleep, chest fall asleep, belly fall asleep, arms fall asleep, hands fall asleep, fingers fall asleep, legs fall asleep, feet fall asleep, toes fall asleep." Overcoming sleep problems takes time and practice. Be patient. For severe sleep problems, see your family physician.

Additional tips for helping your child sleep include setting a regular bedtime routine and time for him to go to sleep; not allowing stimulating play at least one hour or more before bedtime; and having him relax in bed with either reading, listening to music, or talking about things that will not agitate him. Bedtime snacks should be heavier on the carbs than protein to induce sleepiness, and a favorite toy or stuffed animal in bed may comfort him.

Be a role model by showing your child how you use belly breathing in your daily life to relax and to cope with stressful situations. Make belly breathing a family affair; have everyone learn it and you will have less trouble with your child agreeing to practice it. In fact, ask your child, who is now an expert at it, if she would like to teach family members the technique. Teaching your child how to belly breathe provides her with good coping skills that she can use for the rest of her life.

CHAPTER 15

"Be Present" for School Success

T HE VITAL ELEMENTS NEEDED FOR BECOMING A SUCCESSFUL
student are the ability to think, focus, concentrate, and cope with
academic and social pressures in school. Being in school provokes anxiety because students are compared, evaluated, and scored on
their performance. They have to conform to new rules and learn how
to socialize and interact with peers and other adults away from the
safety of parents and home. Students who are anxious about school
often have poor grades, balk at homework, freak out about testing, and
may even avoid socializing with peers.

*Mitch, in second grade, studies for tests, but when he is taking the
test, his anxiety spikes, he panics, and his mind and body shut down
to cope with anxious symptoms, and he can't remember a thing he
studied because "brain freeze" has struck.*

*Isabelle, in fourth grade, is shy, has some social fears, and has
difficulty socializing in a group. The girls she wants to "hang with"
tease her about being so quiet and often leave her out of their
plans. When she tries to be open and talk to them, she fears they
will think she is stupid, so she shuts down and gets quiet.*

Earlier chapters described the excessive worry that creates the distressing anxiety symptoms that make school a miserable experience
for some children and block their normal intellectual and emotional

development. However, the simple technique of "living in the moment" described in this chapter can change your child from a bundle of nerves into a champion student.

Living in the Moment

"Living in the moment," also called "mindfulness," "the here and now," or "being present centered," are phrases commonly used in popular culture. The techniques, based on Eastern philosophy, which includes yoga and martial arts, are in standard use today in stress management skill training, psychiatry/psychotherapy, sports psychology, medicine, and business. Being "present centered," as used in this program, is an easy way to turn off anxiety and to turn on the ability to relax, think clearly, concentrate, and focus, no matter what is happening in the environment.

How Being in the Moment Works

Anxiety is created either by thinking about uncomfortable, embarrassing, scary past experiences and worrying that the events will happen again in the future, or by imagining bad things will occur even though they never have. Anxiety is about the what-ifs: "What if my teacher asks me to go to the board to solve a math problem and I get it wrong and the class laughs at me?" "What if I leave home to go to school and something bad happens to my parents?" "What if I fail my spelling test, again?" "What will I do if my friends won't play with me at recess, like yesterday?" "What will I do if I don't understand my homework and can't finish it?"

By staying squarely in the moment excessive worrying will stop. The moment is the real present. Look at it like this: Each word you read on this page is one moment in time. After you read a word, it is in the past; it's gone (of course you remember it for comprehension). The words coming up in the new paragraph are in the future; they don't exist for you yet. It is only the word you are reading that is in the present. When you live in the moment, the past ceases to exist—bad experiences are no more. And turning off the future will stop the what-ifs, causing anxiety to plummet.

Benefits of Living in the Moment

The benefits of mindfulness have been scientifically studied for decades, and current research is ongoing in complementary and alternative medicine (CAM) centers at major universities and medical centers such as Harvard, Johns Hopkins, Yale, and M.I.T. The evidence points to a wealth of benefits for living in the here and now and includes:

- Increased ability to handle stress and to problem solve
- Increased self-awareness and confidence
- Decreased incidents of anxiety and depression
- Improved concentration, clear thinking, and creativity
- Increased comprehension and understanding of academic material
- Increased ability to relate to others in a positive way

Additional gains include improved functioning of the immune system, a greater ability to handle life changes, an enhanced appreciation of living, and a sense of well-being. Living in the moment won't take away all the stress about going to school or of life in general; nothing can do that. However, using mindfulness will give your child a greater sense of confidence that he can handle and take control of events that before made him feel helpless. It will also teach him important life skills as he grows and makes his way into the world.

Getting to the Moment Is Easy— Staying There Takes Practice

Engaging the mind to focus all attention on what is happening right now, whether it is studying for a test, sitting in class, or trying to interact with peers, is easy—for a few seconds, that is. The trick is to stay in the moment for a good part of the day, or at least during an upsetting experience when anxiety is high and seemingly out of control. Anxiety and its symptoms are powerful and create mental and physical havoc. To be able to use this technique quickly to relieve anxiety and take control of the situation, it will have to be internalized, become a part of your child, become second nature—and that takes time and practice. The same way that you are practicing belly breathing and teaching it to your child is the way you will approach living in the moment. First, you'll have to learn the techniques yourself.

Body Awareness—For Parents

FEEL THE CHAIR

1. Sit in a chair, feet flat on the floor, hands resting in your lap or on the armrests. Breathe easily or do belly breathing. Set a timer for one to two minutes.
2. Close your eyes and focus all of your attention on how your body feels in the chair. Feel your back against the chair, your buttocks and upper thighs on the seat.
3. When thoughts intrude, gently refocus on your body sitting in the chair.
4. When the time is up, sit quietly and see how you feel. Increase practice time as you get more comfortable with the exercise.
5. Repeat this exercise with your eyes open, looking at a point in the room to keep you focused.

FEEL YOUR FEET STANDING/WALKING/RUNNING

1. Set the timer for two minutes.
2. Stand, shoulders back, weight distributed on both legs.
3. Focus all of your attention on how your feet feel in your shoes. Squeeze your toes. How does that feel?

4. Begin to walk slowly, becoming aware of each step, which is one moment in time.
5. Continue walking and gradually increase the pace to fast walking or running, maintaining focus as you go.
6. When thoughts intrude, gently refocus on this exercise.
7. When the time is up, take a few minutes to see how you feel.

Practice body awareness during your daily activities at home and work, for example, while sitting at a desk, walking around your house or at work, and during meals. Practice changing positions from sitting to standing, to walking without breaking concentration.

Now it's time to teach your child.

Explaining Body Awareness to Your Child

Begin the lesson by asking your child to name a few things that concern him and telling him that the worry he has about school will set off a false alarm. Tell your child that you are going to teach him how to prevent the worry, and to stop the false alarm from going off. Best of all, no one will know he is doing it. Make practice times short and fun. Positively reinforce his efforts with praise, hugs and kisses, or time with you. You will need a timer or an alarm clock and a quiet place to practice.

FEEL THE CHAIR

1. Have your child sit in a chair, feet flat on the floor, hands in his lap or on the armrests. Sit next to him.
2. Have him close his eyes. Tell him when his thoughts pull him away from the exercise to toss them into the sky and then to listen closely to what you are saying. Set a timer for one minute.
3. Repeat in a soft voice: "Feel how your back feels on the chair; how your bottom [or any word you use for buttocks] feels sitting on the seat; how your thighs feel on the chair; how your arms feel on the armrests." Repeat until the time is up.

4. Repeat the exercise, but have him open his eyes and focus on a point in the room to keep his concentration from wavering. Continue until the time is up. Ask him how he feels.

FEEL YOUR FEET STANDING/WALKING/RUNNING

1. Have your child stand, shoulders and head relaxed. Set the timer for two minutes. Stand near him.
2. Repeat in a soft voice: "Feel how your feet feel in your shoes, on the floor. Squeeze your toes three times . . . one, two, three. Now start slowly walking around the room, and concentrate on each step as you walk." You can either count the steps, or say something like, "One step, two step, one step, two step," or anything that your child wants you to say.
3. Tell him to walk faster concentrating on how that feels; then have him run in place or around the room for a minute or less. When the time is up, have him tell you how he feels.

ADDITIONAL EXERCISE: FEEL YOUR HANDS

Have your child practice focusing on an item that will fit comfortably in his hands. Ideally it should be smooth, round, and have a little weight to it. When he has mastered that, use other things that he would use in school, such as a pencil, crayon, or pen. Practice while sitting, standing, and walking. If he especially likes something small that he can take to school, it might give him added confidence, but you do want him to be able to use his body to get himself present centered, too.

Practicing in Everyday Living

It's easy to practice with your child in everyday activities so living in the moment will gradually become second nature to him, and will benefit him in school situations. However, you will have to slow your life down, to stop rushing around to teach him this technique. Here are some examples:

During meals teach him to savor his food, focusing on the smell, color, taste, and texture. For example, eat an orange together: Feel its shape, focus on its color, peel it slowly, break apart the sections, and concentrate on the first bite. How does the flesh and juice of the fruit feel? Have him chew slowly focusing on how it feels to eat an orange. Take turns with him telling you his experience and vice versa. Have him focus on a favorite toy, examining it with close attention to its color, shape, and texture.

Practice while doing chores together. When he cleans his room, have him concentrate on each item he picks up and puts away. At the supermarket, have him feel his feet as you both walk down the aisles. What does the handle of the cart feel like? Have him put store items in the cart. What do they look like? How do they feel? Have him wash dishes with you and tell him, "When we do the dishes, we only do the dishes. Feel the plate, the water, the soap, the sponge." Get your whole family living in the moment during work and play and see how good everyone starts to feel.

THE BLINDFOLD GAME

This is a fun game to increase attention and to learn to use the senses other than sight to stay in the moment. Blindfold your child and place a number of things in her hands from food to toys. Set a timer for thirty seconds for each item. Have her concentrate and use smell, touch, and/or taste to guess what each object is. She can also race against the clock to see how many items she can correctly identify before the alarm goes off.

Practice at Home—Body Awareness Clinic

Following are exercises that will help your child overcome anxiety in a variety of school situations and also teach your child to "be in the moment" in any stressful situation.

GOING TO SCHOOL

The night before school, have your child use the body awareness exercises coupled with belly breathing as soon as anxious thoughts about school occur. On school mornings, as soon as your child gets out of bed, have her focus on her feet or anything she is doing or touching while getting ready—for example, the feel of her clothing, putting on her shoes, or eating breakfast. She feels the seat while riding the bus, and she feels her feet while walking into school and walking into class. As soon as she sits at her desk, she feels the seat. Or she focuses on something she is holding in her hand. If separation anxiety is severe, do as many practice runs as necessary when school is out.

STUDYING FOR A TEST

Set up a desk and chair in the house to make a home schoolroom. Have your child sit down and belly breathe for a few minutes before he begins studying. As soon as thoughts come into his mind, have him toss them to the sky and tell him to "feel the chair" for a few seconds or "feel the book or worksheet," then gently turn his attention back to studying. Repeat as needed until he finishes studying. In Chapter 8, follow the instructions in the Overcoming Test Anxiety Clinic to set up a similar format for using body awareness exercises for studying.

TEST TAKING

The night before a test, tell your child that as soon as he thinks about the upcoming test he is to focus on his body or something tangible to turn off worry. When he goes to bed have him "feel the bed" while belly breathing before he goes to sleep. When he wakes the next morning, he is to belly breathe. When he arises, he is to immediately focus on his feet. Throughout the morning whenever he thinks about the test he is to turn off the future by focusing on something else. Riding to school he will focus on sitting, walking into school focus on his feet, sitting in the classroom focus on sitting or on his pencil or something on his desk. A good technique is to put both arms flat on the desk and "feel the desk" while belly breathing.

Practice mock tests at home with you as the teacher handing him a test while he breathes and focuses and completes the test in the time he would have at school. Get old tests from the teacher if possible, or make up your own from homework assignments. See Chapter 8, "My Child Has Test Anxiety," for study and test-taking skills.

BEING CALLED ON IN CLASS/GOING TO THE BOARD

Hang a blackboard in your home classroom. Have your child sit at his desk breathing and feeling the chair while you, the teacher, call on him to do work at the board. As soon as he stands up, have him "feel his feet" as he walks to the board. Continue to play the teacher and call on him to answer a question in class. When he hears his name, he is to squeeze his toes once to cut off any worry that begins, exhale slowly, and try to answer. Practice asking him some questions he might stumble over or not know and have him rehearse saying, "I don't know the answer," while staying relaxed and present centered. Remind him to belly breathe, too.

PEER RELATIONSHIPS AND SOCIAL ANXIETY

Tell your child that together you are going to help him feel more comfortable when he is with classmates and peers by using body awareness. First, your child has to be practiced in the body awareness and belly-breathing exercises. Next, you want to write down exactly how he feels about socializing and what he is thinking about when he is with other children. For example, does he feel that they don't like him? Is he afraid to sound stupid? Is he afraid to be teased? Is he afraid of confrontation? Does he feel awkward around peers? Also, try to observe him in action with other children. What is his body language? What does he say, or not say? Does he make and sustain eye contact? Have your child in a relaxed state when you question him because these questions may upset him and he may be reluctant to answer. Question him while you're having fun, for example, when you're playing a game together or taking a walk. This way your talk won't seem confrontational and he will be more open to expressing his feelings.

With your child, make a plan of action in your Overcoming School Anxiety Journal. Break down his social fears so they are manageable and achievable, working on one issue at a time, for example, staying in the moment while increasing eye contact or starting conversations. Don't rush things; go slow and steady because you do not want to set him up for failure. With your child, decide where he is going to use body awareness; then role-play the scenarios with him. Let him determine when the time is right for him to try these techniques around other children.

Rehearsing in mock situations is important. It readies your child for the real situation, reducing the what-ifs and worry. Practice using all of the exercises prior to the real experiences in role-play with either you, another trusted adult, or a sibling. Using guided imagery to picture the dreaded situation while imagining himself coping with it, being relaxed, and feeling confident is another way for him to master his anxiety.

CHAPTER 16

Learning to Let Go and Flow

Ꮗ

NO MATTER THE CAUSE OF SCHOOL ANXIETY, THE DISTRESS-
ing symptoms of an anxiety attack leave a child feeling out of
control and helpless. When that happens, the most common
coping method is to disengage from the environment to deal with the
panic, thereby making the ability to concentrate almost impossible.

> *Marisa, a fourth grader, goes into a panic whenever she has to read
> aloud in class. When she's called on, she gets an adrenaline rush,
> her heart pounds, and she feels dizzy. She tries to push the panic
> down, but that only increases her anxiety, which decreases her abil-
> ity to concentrate, making her stumble and lose her place while
> she's reading.*

> *Terry, in sixth grade, is very anxious about agreeing to sing a solo in
> the choral spring concert. Last year, he soloed, but it was a mortify-
> ing experience. When he opened his mouth to sing, he panicked,
> froze, and could not remember the words. He wants to solo this
> year, but when he thinks of doing it he worries about forgetting the
> words and his heart pounds.*

The first instinct for most sufferers of panic is to cope by fighting
the fear, emotionally burying symptoms. It is the white-knuckle defense. The reasoning is, "If I don't think about it, and tighten up to
push feelings away, then my panic will go away." That's what Marisa

and Terry did. They froze and became rock solid when their panic hit, desperately wanting to turn off those scary feelings, and who can blame them? In the end, they turned off their brain's ability to think, remember, and reason. No wonder she stumbles and loses her place, and he can't think of the words to the song.

The white-knuckle defense against anxiety doesn't work. It only makes things worse because it increases tension. The best way for your child to stop anxiety from preventing him from having an enjoyable and successful experience in school is for him to accept and face his fear, ride it out, then let it go.

Don't Fight the Fear

Learning how to relax and be present centered are wonderful methods to use to reduce anxiety. However, it is the ability to stop fighting against the fear or trying to bury frightening physical and emotional manifestations of anxiety that is the more powerful coping mechanism. Riding out the storm by actually staying connected to the distressing symptoms will decrease their hold. It is about not being afraid of being afraid. It's tough to do this, to go toe to toe with fear, relax into it, and not care that anxiety is present. But it can be done and you can help your child learn how to do it.

Letting Go of Fear Is Not Just Relaxing

In order to benefit from the exercises in this chapter, your child has to be able to relax quickly using breathing techniques and turn off worry by being present centered. The technique of accepting and then letting go of fear and symptoms of anxiety has deeper meaning than just relaxing. It is a profound emotional change that must take place for anxiety to really lose its control over mind and body. If a deep belief exists that the symptoms of anxiety in all of their disturbing manifestations are harmless, that it does not matter where or when they strike, anxiety and panic will decline and lose their power.

Maddie, a fifth grader, suffered from severe test anxiety in most subjects. She chronically worried because at least once a week she had to take a quiz or test, which she generally did poorly on. When Maddie learned how to face her fear, let it be, and then let go of it, things changed. It took time and practice, but she got to the point that she believed, "I don't care if I have a panic attack during the math test because I can ride it out. I studied and can still do well!" Guess what happened? Her panic decreased, and over time her confidence increased. And when she did get panicky, although it felt uncomfortable she knew it was nothing more than a lot of symptoms that couldn't hurt her. Eventually Maddie's panic will be infrequent, or not happen at all.

How to Face Fear and Go with the Flow

So how do you get your frightened child to stop fighting anxiety and give in to it? It will take patience and lots of practice. Dr. Claire Weekes (1903–1990), an Australian physician, pioneered cures for anxiety, agoraphobia, and panic through a program of total acceptance of the fear. In her book *More Help for Your Nerves*, Dr. Weekes laid out an anxiety recovery program that includes:

- *Facing Fear.* Admit the fear, but healing is possible too. It is critical not to avoid the circumstances and situations that cause panic.
- *Accepting Fear.* Learn how to loosen the body as much as possible when panic hits to decrease tension. Remain in the feared situation.
- *Floating Through Fear.* Instead of fighting panic, relax into it and ride it out.
- *Giving It Time.* Overcoming anxiety takes time, so be patient but persistent.

Emotions that are uncomfortable, such as fear or anger, cannot be avoided, erased, or thought away. They are part of what makes us human. When we disconnect from our feelings, we disconnect from ourselves and from our life. By facing and accepting all of our feelings, including fear, we stay in the present, connected to what is happening, making it possible to cope, think, and take action.

You do not want your child disconnecting emotionally in school because of his anxiety. You want him to be present, no matter how he feels, so he can learn and develop normally. Going with the flow will teach him how to do that. Before you can teach your child the exercises in this chapter, you need to do each one yourself.

Creating a List of Fears

Tell your child that together you are going to make a list of the things or situations that cause him anxiety, and then you are going to teach him how to stop being anxious when those things occur by learning how to let go of anxiety. To begin, either write what he tells you or have him write it himself. Then have him rate his level of anxiety for each thing on the list using the following School Anxiety Scale. Young children may not be able to do this exercise, so you will have to test it on them. Or, use the variation on creating a feared scene. If your child adamantly refuses to do these exercises, or doesn't understand them, delete them from your program, but try again when he matures.

School Anxiety Scale

10_____Panic land!! It's out of control!

09_____Help! It's running away with me!

08_____I can't stop it!

07_____It's here!

06_____I'm not feeling good.

05_____It's building up inside.

04_____Uh-oh!

03_____I feel a little bad.

02_____It's still okay.

01_____I feel good.

0_____No school anxiety in sight.

MAKING THE LIST

Make a list of his feared scenes and then have him rate them on the School Anxiety Scale following these examples:

1. I feel like I'm going to faint when my teacher calls me up to the board. Scale rating: 10
2. My brain freezes when the teacher hands out test papers: Scale rating: 7
3. I feel nervous every time I walk through the school doors. I get stomach cramps and feel like I'm going to throw up. Scale rating: 8

Having him rate his level of anxiety will help your child understand that anxiety is not static, that it goes up and down throughout the anxiety-producing event. Also, by having him rate his anxiety prior to the exercise, then after it, he will see that he can take control of his anxiety, and eventually beat it. Remember to keep practice time short and if your child wants to stop, do so, and continue later or the next day. Practice all exercises at least three times a week. Increase practice time gradually to ten minutes or more. These exercises are hard to do, so remember to praise your child's efforts.

VARIATION: MAKING THE FEARED SCENE TANGIBLE

Since children often communicate and express themselves easier through play, especially if your child has trouble picturing her feared scene, suggest that she create it through any of the following mediums:

drawing; painting; sculpting; building with blocks or Legos; making a three-dimensional scene out of paper; or setting up the scene using playhouses, toy figures, and accessories.

After the scene is created, ask your child how she feels about it. When she looks at the scene, does she get anxious? When she thinks about herself in the scene how anxious does she get? Then have her rate it on the School Anxiety Scale. Tell her you are going to teach her how to feel relaxed and calm when she looks at or thinks about the scene, but not now. Put the created scene in a safe place, and do the exercises either later in the day or the next day. As she finishes working through one feared scene, have her create the next fear, and so on, until she is comfortable in every situation. If you have the room, put each scene away after it is worked on, because anxiety comes and goes, and she may have to revisit working on the same scenes for quite a while.

Learning to Let Go—Loosening Your Body

Loosening is being able to release all body tension, mentally and physically, and become like a rag doll, or a piece of cooked spaghetti. It is a part of learning to "let go." The prerequisite is knowing how to belly breathe. You will need a timer plus a rag doll or a strand of cooked spaghetti.

1. Have your child lie down or sit in a comfortable chair and belly breathe.
2. Hand him the rag doll or spaghetti strand. Let him touch it and examine it. Tell him you want him to loosen his body so he feels like the doll or the pasta. Set the timer for two to three minutes.
3. Have him close his eyes and belly breathe while you say slowly in a soft voice, "Relax your head, neck, and shoulders; relax your back; relax your chest; relax your arms, hands, fingers; relax your belly, your legs, feet, and toes. Feel all the tension flow out when you breathe."
4. Repeat until the time is up. Ask him if he feels like the doll or spaghetti. The goal is for your child to relax and loosen quickly at will.

Floating—Riding the Wave of Anxiety

Floating is the ability to ride out the anxiety, soar above it, no matter how severe the symptoms are, thereby rendering it powerless. To begin, ask your child what he pictures in his mind and feels when he closes his eyes and thinks of floating. If he can swim, ask him to think how it feels when he floats on the water, or rides a wave to the shore if he has done that. Or what he imagines it feels like to float in the air like a butterfly, or a cloud.

LEARNING TO FLOAT

1. Have your child lie down and belly breathe, eyes closed. Set the timer for two to three minutes.
2. Say to him in a soft, calm voice, "Relax your head, neck, and shoulders; relax your back; relax your belly, your arms, your hands, and your fingers; relax your legs, feet, and toes. Keep breathing and relaxing, feeling tension flowing out of your body, breathing, relaxing, flowing." Continue until he relaxes.
3. Tell him to imagine his floating picture, to see himself floating, feeling relaxed, calm, and loose. Say to him, "When you float, you are above all the anxious feelings that scare you. They are still there, but they can't hurt you or stop you from doing anything you want to do, and do well." After the exercise is finished, ask him how he feels.

LETTING GO AND FLOATING

Explain to your child that you are going to ask him to imagine one of the feared situations you helped him write down, or a tangible one, and then he will loosen and float, instead of trying to make the anxiety go away. Tell him he may feel uncomfortable, but you are here, and he is safe. Ask if he agrees to get anxious. Let him choose which fear to work on first.

LETTING GO AND FLOATING—LYING DOWN

1. Have your child lie down.
2. Tell him to close his eyes and either read his feared scene to him or have him picture it. Ask him to see himself in the scene and to try to feel all the emotions, the tension, and the fear. Ask him to nod if he feels anxious. If he doesn't, give him another minute, and then continue the exercise.
3. When his anxiety surfaces, he is to belly breathe and at the same time he is to let his feelings stay up on the surface, and to loosen his body and think about being the butterfly, or floating in the water, or whatever his image of floating is. He is to see himself floating on top of the anxiety, riding out the waves of symptoms. The anxiety is under him, but he floats on top, so it can't hurt him. Remind him not to fight the feelings. Repeat in a calm voice, "Breathe, relax, flow, float, loosen."
4. Continue until the anxiety lessens. Rate his anxiety on the School Anxiety Scale.
5. When you finish, have him relax and ask him how he feels. Tell him it will take time and practice to float through anxiety quickly, but he will succeed at it.

VARIATION: USING THE TANGIBLE FEARED SCENE

Either move the feared scene your child has created to him or place a soft mat on the floor next to the scene. First, have him sit or stand and look at the scene, touch the scene, trying to get his anxiety up. Rate how he feels on the School Anxiety Scale. Then have him lie down, close his eyes, and follow the previous exercise.

LETTING GO AND FLOATING—SITTING

1. Have your child sit in a chair, eyes closed.
2. He can hold the doll or spaghetti strand. Tell him to picture his feared scene and loosen his body. Say in a calm voice,

"Belly breathe; let all tension flow out of your body. Relax your head, neck, and shoulders; relax your back and chest; relax your belly, arms, hands, and fingers; relax your legs, feet, and toes." Repeat until you see he is relaxed.

3. Now, keeping the feared scene in his mind, have him float. Tell him, "Ride out the anxiety. Don't fight it. Float above the feelings that scare you; they can't hurt you. Loosen and float, loosen and float," until he feels the anxiety lessen. Ask him how he feels. Practice the sitting exercise with his eyes open, too. Have him rate his anxiety on the School Anxiety Scale.

VARIATION: USING THE TANGIBLE FEARED SCENE

Either move the feared scene your child has created to him, or place a chair next to it. First, have him sit or stand and look at the scene, touch the scene, trying to get his anxiety up. Have him rate how he feels on the School Anxiety Scale. Then, have him sit down, close his eyes, and follow the previous exercise.

LETTING GO AND FLOATING—STANDING/WALKING

1. Have your child stand. She can hold either the rag doll or spaghetti. Stand near her.
2. Tell her to picture her feared scene—feeling the emotions and getting anxious.
3. Now, say to her in a soft, calm voice, "Belly breathe; feel all tension flow out of your body. Relax your head, neck, and shoulders; relax your chest, back, arms, hands, fingers, belly, legs, feet, toes. You feel like the doll [or spaghetti]." Repeat until she relaxes.
4. Now, tell her to float, to ride out the wave of fear, to rise above it. Say to her, "See yourself floating on top of the anxiety; it cannot hurt you." Tell her to continue loosening and floating until the anxiety subsides.

5. When the exercise is finished, ask her how she feels, and rate it on the School Anxiety Scale.

VARIATION: USING THE TANGIBLE FEARED SCENE

First, have your child look at the scene, touch the scene, trying to get her anxiety up. Have her rate how she feels on the School Anxiety Scale. Then, have her stand next to her scene and follow the previous exercise.

When and Where to Practice

Do mock practices in the home schoolroom and at school when it is closed or on weekends. Ask school officials if your child can practice in school, too, when it is open after students are gone for the day. Examples of mock practices are leaving home to go to school, walking through the school doors, walking into the classroom, sitting at a desk, being in class and having the classroom door closed, test taking, and going to the board. If your child has social fears, role-play how to overcome the feared scene.

Adding Calming Statements

When your child is able to let go and float, you can have her add calming and positive phrases that oppose her fears. For example, while she lets go and floats, she can say to herself things like: "I'm very anxious about taking this test, but my feelings can't stop me from doing well on it" or "I'm panicking because I don't know anyone in this new school, but I can float above it and nothing will happen" or "I can breathe and calm myself while I'm waiting for the teacher to call me to the board."

Work together with your child to come up with sentences that have meaning. Have her repeat the motivating and opposing fear statements so they will begin to replace the negative mental tapes that accompany anxiety. For more information on counteracting negative self-talk, see Chapter 10, "Building Your Child's Self-Esteem."

Troubleshooting

If your child balks at letting go and floating, don't push it. Mentally bringing up his fears may be too uncomfortable. Continue having him practice the breathing and staying-in-the-moment exercises. When he has mastered those, reintroduce the letting-go exercises without the feared scenes. Only when he can relax and loosen very quickly should you reintroduce floating. If he still balks, don't have him pull up his feared scenes; plan to do the mock practices instead.

Letting go and going with the flow are only one aspect of the Overcoming School Anxiety Program, but a powerful one, especially when combined with breathing, staying in the moment, and the other anxiety-busting techniques in this book. The goal is for your child to emotionally internalize the idea that anxiety symptoms, although distressing and disturbing, cannot hurt him or block his success. When he believes that, nothing can stop him.

CHAPTER 17

Eat Right to Feel Right

ɢ∿

W HAT CHILDREN FUEL THEIR BODIES WITH HAS A MAJOR effect on their ability to handle stress and the anxiety created by it. Some foods and substances found in food can increase anxiety, while others can decrease it. The intake of processed and junk foods creates mind and body stress, and a risk of anxiety, depression, vitamin and mineral deficiencies, and other physical and mental conditions.

John, a fifth grader with test anxiety, refuses to eat breakfast because thinking about the day's upcoming math quiz has upset his stomach. However, on the school bus he shares his friend's donut and Pepsi. By the time John gets to school, he is having a sugar high, increasing his anxiety level. However, within thirty minutes of the high, John experiences the sugar crash, making him feel fatigued and reducing his ability to think and handle the stress of the math quiz.

Jessie, in fourth grade, is overweight by thirty pounds and refuses to eat most vegetables, lean meats, and whole grains. She lives on chicken nuggets, burgers, fries, and noodles. Jessie is teased regularly about her size, making her anxious about going to school. She also demonstrates poor coping skills in handling the stress of homework and tests. Jessie has low self-worth and has lost her motivation to learn, participate in class, and socialize. She has been labeled an underachiever by her teacher, and spends most of her time at home on the computer, watching TV, and snacking on junk food.

This chapter will discuss why good nutrition is basic to a holistic plan for overcoming school anxiety. Guidelines are included to help you get your child interested in healthy eating, and Kristin Kwak, MS, RD, LDN, a licensed nutritionist, gives you ideas for healthy, good-tasting meals, school lunches, and snacks. Consult with your family physician or a nutritionist before using the information in this chapter.

How Does Food Affect My Child's Stress Level and Moods?

There is an old saying that "you are what you eat." Ongoing research over the years supports the fact that mood can be effected by the type of foods we eat, by certain additives in food, or by a lack of vitamins and minerals in our diets. Proper diet and nutrition are an essential component to any holistic treatment of stress, anxiety, or other conditions affecting success in school. Children's brains develop at a fast pace and poor nutrition can block healthy brain function and growth. Fueling your child with nourishing food will make him feel good physically, will keep his mind functioning at its peak, and will increase his ability to handle stressful situations in school.

What Is Food?

Food is a combination of chemicals that are derived from natural sources: plants and animals. Food is made up of three macro (large) nutrients: carbohydrates, proteins, and fats. Carbohydrates provide fiber and are the primary source of energy. Protein builds and repairs muscle tissue, helps fight infection, and helps ensure hair and nail growth. Fats provide essential fatty acids and a concentrated source of energy. Micro (small) nutrients, like vitamins and minerals, aid in chemical and hormonal processes in the body.

Food takes many forms today. Natural or whole foods, like fruits, vegetables, brown rice, organic chicken, and dairy products free of bovine growth hormone (BGH), haven't been altered and retain their primary qualities and nutritional value. Processed foods have been changed or altered in some way by food manufacturers. Let's look at the foods and substances that could lead to poor nutrition and the development of negative mental and physical conditions if not eaten in moderation.

What Is Junk Food?

Today we live in a fast-paced, fast-food world. Millions of American children eat fast food at least once a day, while TV ads entice children to beg for foods that are loaded with sugar, fat, and salt. Junk food is any food that has little or no nutritional value (low in essential vitamins, minerals, and fiber) but contains an excess of fat, calories, salt, and sugar. Foods considered "junk" are soft drinks; chips; candy; and fast foods such as fries, burgers, and shakes.

Processed foods such as sweetened cold cereals or several types of crackers deliver high quantities of sugar and salt and can be just as unhealthful as junk food. A diet high in junk food and low in whole food can be linked to vitamin deficiencies, obesity, and other serious physical and mental health problems. Junk food also contains additives to enhance taste and texture, making them attractive to children. Let's look at how some major components of junk food impact children's anxiety levels and school performance.

Sugar

It's hard to go down a supermarket aisle these days and find foods that do not contain sugar. Some sugar is found naturally in foods, like fruit, but processed foods often contain an excess of added sugar to help make them taste preferable to their less-sweet, natural, whole-food counterparts. Some processed foods are obviously high in sugar, like candy, desserts, soft drinks, powdered drinks, and sugar-sweetened cereals. However, some foods contain hidden sugar, like ketchup, mayonnaise, bread, tomato sauces, barbeque sauce, fruit snacks, and fruit juice drinks.

Sugar has calories but no nutritional value, and contains no vitamins or minerals. When you eat sugar, the body metabolizes it quickly. It is absorbed into the bloodstream and immediately produces a "sugar high," followed by a "sugar low." If your child is overloading on soft drinks, candy, or other foods high in sugar, the fight-or-flight syndrome may be triggered because sugar significantly increases the manufacture of adrenaline, which may produce symptoms such as rapid heartbeat, headaches, irritability, jitteriness, and difficulty in concentrating. Large quantities of sugar do not contribute to hyperactivity but can exacerbate mood instability, symptoms of anxiety, depression, ADHD, and physical illnesses.

Salt

Salt, a natural mineral found in underground salt deposits and seawater, is necessary for health. It is used as a preservative, for pharmacological uses, and to enhance the flavor of food. Today, salt is an important ingredient in modern food processing because it adds taste and texture to food, stops the growth of harmful microorganisms, and cures meat. However, ingesting too much salt can lead to the development of high blood pressure and the depletion of potassium. Potassium, a mineral important for the normal functioning of the nervous system, makes sure cells and muscles function properly, keeps blood pressure low, and helps balance body fluids. So, it's wise to limit salt intake.

Excess Calories

There is an epidemic of childhood obesity in the United States, and experts agree that most cases are caused by diet, yet we are a culture obsessed with thinness. Along with this epidemic is the onset of type 2 diabetes in children at an alarming rate. Children whose diets are based on junk foods are at an increased risk of not meeting their nutrient needs, yet exceeding their energy needs. In other words, they don't get adequate vitamins, minerals, and fiber but end up with far too many calories. This puts them at risk of decreased physical fitness, obesity, diabetes, and cardiovascular disease. It also decreases their ability to focus, concentrate, and remember important information.

Fats

Fats are naturally found in whole foods like meats, fish, eggs, and plant sources such as nuts and seeds, olives, and avocados. Oils derived from plant sources like olive oil, canola oil, and corn oil are natural fats we eat and cook with. Butter is also a natural fat. In moderation, these fat sources provide children's bodies with essential fatty acids and energy that they need for normal growth and development. On the other hand, the fats most often used in processed and junk foods are hydrogenated and saturated fats, like hydrogenated vegetable shortening, margarine, and lard. A diet based on processed and junk foods promotes heart disease, type 2 diabetes, and obesity. Limit your child's intake of fats from processed, junk, and fast foods, and focus on moderate amounts of healthier fats from natural plant sources.

Low-Fiber Foods

Fiber is usually completely missing in junk foods! Fiber is important for a healthy digestive system, for promoting normal blood cholesterol and sustained blood sugar levels (which will help avoid mood swings), and for controlling weight. Plant foods are excellent sources of fiber, especially all fruits and vegetables and whole-grain products like oatmeal, whole-wheat bread, rye bread, and whole-wheat pasta. While your child is in the transition stage of beginning to eat more fruits and vegetables, unflavored soluble fiber can be purchased and added to drinks and foods such as cereals and hamburger.

Processed Foods

Approximately three quarters of food in the Western world is processed. Foods are processed for a number of reasons: to preserve and extend shelf life, to kill harmful bacteria, to make cooking time faster and easier, and to make food more digestible. These are all good reasons. However, processing also decreases the nutritional value of food. For example, when whole grains are processed, the natural fiber and nutrients in the whole grain are removed, and then some nutrients are added back to the processed grain. The end result is a product inferior to its natural state.

Additionally, food manufacturers add excess amounts of salt, sugar, and fat to improve taste and texture, which may make it tastier but less nutritious. Take a look at a can of vegetable soup next time you shop, and you'll often find it contains 500 milligrams or more of sodium per serving! So, whenever possible, read food labels and choose whole foods.

Preservatives and Additives

In addition to salt, sugar, and fat, other food additives can spell trouble for your child. These additives include BHA; BHT; sulfites, such as sulfur dioxide; food dyes, such as FD&C Blue No. 1; monosodium glutamate (MSG); and acesulfame-K. Preservatives and additives can cause chemical or allergic reactions that have been linked to mental and physical conditions that include headaches or migraines, stomach upsets, anxiety, depression, hyperactivity in children, skin rashes or hives, and sleep problems. Other conditions being studied are the development of asthma, irritable bowel syndrome, and some cancers.

How Does Nutrition Affect My Child's Brain?

All physical and mental functions are controlled by the brain such as movement, thought processes, and emotions. Neurotransmitters, nerve cells, are the main communication system between mind and body, and keep everything working. Children develop cognitively even into their teens, so good nutrition is crucial for their normal development. Poor nutrition can negatively affect the production of neurotransmitters, such as serotonin, which has a calming effect, and dopamine and norepinephrine, both responsible for the ability to think, concentrate, and remember. Ultimately and over time, this diminished brain function can lead to anxiety states, depression, and poor coping skills.

The brain needs lots of energy for it to work properly and at its peak. Did you know your brain consumes 30 percent of your daily caloric intake? A poorly nourished brain affects the entire nervous system and can lead to a high risk of emotional problems. The brain needs vitamins, minerals, glucose, and other chemicals, obtained from a good diet. However, supplements such as vitamins are important too, especially if processed foods are part of a daily diet.

What Are the Vitamins and Minerals My Child Needs?

Vitamins are found naturally in foods and are crucial for proper brain function and general good health. Since the body cannot manufacture most vitamins, they must be found in the foods that we eat. How important are vitamins? Studies show that even small deficiencies can affect mental and physical health, which can lead to negative physical and mental conditions. A number of vitamins and minerals play an important role in reducing stress and anxiety.

B Vitamins

B1 (thiamine) is for energy. Deficiencies cause fatigue, anxiety, loss of concentration, depression, insomnia, and stomach problems. B3 (niacin) also increases energy and is vital for a balanced nervous system. Deficiencies lead to agitation and anxiety. B6 (pyridoxine) helps create neurotransmitters and aids in building blood cells and antibodies. B12 (cobalamin) aids in creating red blood cells, proper functioning of the nervous system, and is important for memory and concentration. Foods high in B vitamins include whole grains, legumes, nuts, seeds, lean meats, poultry, fish, and whole-grain cereals.

Vitamin C and Other Vitamins

Vitamin C (ascorbic acid) is an antioxidant and aids in mental functions and wound healing and preventing allergic reactions. Vitamins A and D build healthy bones and teeth. Vitamin E is vital for proper circulation, and for healthy red blood cells and strong muscles. Vitamin K is necessary for blood clotting. Foods high in vitamin C are strawberries, citrus fruits, potatoes, and red peppers. Dairy products fortified with vitamin D are excellent sources of calcium and vitamin D, while nuts, seeds, and plant-based oils are sources of vitamin E.

Minerals

Minerals are nonorganic substances that aid in the assimilation of vitamins and help build new cells. There are over sixty minerals in the body, which are found in bones, blood, nerves, muscle, and tissue. Deficiencies can lead to mental conditions such as anxiety, poor life-coping skills, and depression. Important minerals are magnesium, which aids in relaxing muscles and calming nerves; iron, which carries oxygen to the cells in our body to give us energy; potassium, which helps neurotransmitters communicate from brain to body and vice versa; and zinc, for sharp mental processes and overall health.

✎ Guidelines for Getting Your Child to Love Healthful Foods

Getting your child to eat in a healthful way will be easier the younger your child is. Nevertheless, even if you have to make major changes with an older child, it is worth the effort and can be done with some hard work and patience. The changes in your child's eating habits may have to be done slowly and over time, because your child may initially resist. Be consistent and supportive by providing your child with plenty of fruits; vegetables; whole-grain foods; and lean meats, poultry, and fish on a daily basis. Purchase and allow convenience junk and fast foods only occasionally. Remember, you provide and control what your child eats. If you provide healthful choices, you'll be less likely to deal with complications of poor nutrition. Be determined, stay the course, and your persistence will eventually pay off.

1. Make healthy eating a family affair.
2. Be a role model for your child—check out your own diet.
3. Educate yourself about your family's nutritional needs.
4. Choose whole fresh foods at least 80 percent of the time.
5. Get your child involved in shopping and cooking—give him choices; make it fun.

6. Pack a healthy school lunch—have your child help.
7. Join with other parents to make your child's school offer healthy lunches.
8. Have healthy snacks available at home.
9. Teach your child to drink water and occasionally fruit juices instead of soda.
10. Eat together as a family as often as possible with good food and good talk.

The U.S. Department of Agriculture has information about the nutritional needs of children by ages. It also features interactive games, posters, worksheets, and other materials that children will enjoy at MyPyramid.gov.

What's That About Bananas Reducing Anxiety?

Bananas are often used by some musicians to conquer performance anxiety. They state that eating one or two bananas about thirty minutes prior to a performance reduces the symptoms of stage fright, which include heart palpitations, shaking, and loss of concentration. Although no scientific studies have been done regarding this phenomenon, it is believed that bananas work because they contain potassium and other substances that act like beta-blockers, which "block" the effects of stress hormones, such as adrenaline and cortisol. The thick, creamy consistency of bananas also helps to relieve the stomach upset associated with anxiety. If your child is anxious on test days, try giving him a banana.

Which Health Professionals Can Help My Child?

You can start off with your family physician or pediatrician, who can give you information on your child's nutritional needs or refer you to a dietary expert, dietician, or nutritionist. Homeopathic doctors, nurses with specialties in nutrition, chiropractors, and other alternative medicine practitioners can guide you, too.

Kristin Kwak's Sample Menus and Healthy-Eating Tips

"Parents are responsible for determining what their children eat, while kids are responsible for determining how much they eat."

—ELLYN SATTER, RD, ACSW

Children are born with the ability to determine when they are hungry and when they are full. When a variety of healthy food is offered, the child will naturally choose and consume the adequate amount for her normal growth and development. When junk food is the predominate choice, the ability to determine fullness is often impaired. Thus, overeating and being overweight result. For optimum health and to keep your child at or return her to her natural, healthy weight, focus on including fruit and vegetables in at least two meals or snacks every day. Balance these out with whole grains, lean protein choices, and healthful fats. Here are examples of healthful meals and snacks.

Breakfast Choices

Try to include fruit, whole grains, and a dairy product or lean protein. Choose fresh, dried, or canned fruit (aim for one piece or a half cup), 100 percent fruit juices; whole-grain cereals with at least five grams of fiber (read labels); whole-wheat pancakes, oatmeal, grits, Cream of Wheat; 1 percent or skim milk, low-fat yogurt; one to two eggs (hard boiled, poached, or prepared using healthful oils), lean ham, or Canadian bacon.

Lunch Choices

Focus on getting a fruit and vegetable at every lunch. Choose 100 percent fruit juice boxes; fresh, canned, or dried fruit; baby carrots; precut vegetables and low-fat dip or peanut butter; shelf-stable dairy drinks containing 30 percent calcium or a half cup of natural or organic yogurt; low-fat string cheese; sandwiches made with deli turkey, lean ham, or lean roast beef; small bagel with low-fat cream cheese; vegetable, tomato, or chicken noodle soup with whole-grain crackers.

After-School Snack Choices

This is a great opportunity to get in another fruit or vegetable. For variety, try vegetables and low-fat dip or fruit cut and dipped into flavored yogurt. Yogurt-fruit smoothies or vanilla yogurt and low-fat granola are also great choices. Low-fat microwave popcorn or low-fat cheese and crackers and 100 percent fruit juice can be quick and easy. Homemade banana, pumpkin, raisin, pineapple, and apple quick breads or muffins with a glass of low-fat milk will also satisfy after-school hunger.

Dinner Choices

Dinner should comprise the last one-fifth of the day's energy or calorie needs. It is often the largest meal, yet it is eaten after we've burned up most of our day's calories. To help mitigate overeating at dinner, make sure the meal includes protein, whole-grain carbohydrates, vegetables, and healthy fats. Limit fried and breaded meats, fish, and poultry, and choose grilled, sautéed, broiled, or baked methods most often. Include potatoes, pasta, rice, or bread in their most natural form, with small amounts of added olive oil, butter, or sauces. Avoid heavy cream sauce, cheese sauces, or potatoes that are deep fried. Fresh, frozen, or no-salt-added canned vegetables should be eaten at every dinner—two different vegetables or two servings is even better! Serve vegetables plain or seasoned with herbs; refrain from adding too much fat, salt, or sauce.

Desserts

Including a dessert can be an important part of a meal, especially on a special event. On a regular or daily basis, fruit or low-fat yogurt is a wise choice. Healthy choices like oatmeal and molasses cookies made with healthy fats or low-fat ice cream, frozen yogurt, sherbet, or sorbet can also serve to complete a meal. Reserve cakes, regular ice cream, cookies (especially store-bought types), and other high-fat desserts for special occasions.

CHAPTER 18

Getting Physical with Your Child

❧

Decades of research by the U.S. Government, the World Health Organization, and health research centers have concluded that physical exercise is positively linked to a state of mental well-being. The Overcoming School Anxiety Program is a holistically oriented, proactive approach to treating the whole child, not just symptoms, and physical activity or exercise is an important part of the program.

> *Kristen, a kindergartner, never wanted to leave home to start school. After five months of school, she would still cry and hold on to her mother's leg when she had to leave home. Her parents are adamant that she go, but the tantrums are wearing them down. By chance, her mother's yoga school started a class for children and moms. Kristen was signed up and has been going to yoga class for the past month. Through yoga breathing and exercises, Kristen is learning to relax and going to school is getting better by the day.*

In this chapter you will find out why physical exercise is helpful in conquering anxiety, the types of activities and exercises you can explore with your child, and guidelines for beginning an exercise program for your child, yourself, and your family. Consult with your family physician before allowing your child to participate in a physical exercise program.

Put Exercise at the Top of Your Child's School Anxiety Program

Your school-anxious child has to deal with the chronic stress of navigating the school environment five days a week, and about eight hours a day. That's a lot to handle. Your child might already be showing signs of school stress with poor grades, school refusal, low self-esteem, fears of peer relationships, and daily unhappiness.

Although not a panacea, regular physical activity can help your child to handle stress positively, to become physically and mentally stronger, to increase concentration, and to build confidence in social arenas. So, turn off the TV and computer, and get physical with your child.

We Were Meant to Move

Our bodies were meant to be active—to walk, to run, to do manual labor, to work off the stress of living. But today we live in a sedentary culture. Most of us work at desks over forty hours a week, drive instead of walk, and spend little time doing physical activities in our daily lives. We have to join gyms or make special time to work out to get in any exercise at all during the day. This lifestyle shows in our high rates of stress-induced physical and mental conditions.

In today's culture, children work by going to school; most don't labor on farms anymore. Some children participate in sports, but most lead sedentary lives, too, sitting in school all day, then going home to spend hours passively watching TV or playing on the computer. When children get anxious about school, most don't have a chance to physically work the stress out of their system, but carry it inside, which could lead to high levels of anxiety and a host of other mental conditions, such as depression.

Let's review the fight-or-flight response again to see how it affects mind and body, and why physical activity can help counter it. When a child gets anxious, say about leaving home to go to school, test taking, or socializing with peers, the fight-or-flight reaction kicks into gear. In an instant, stress hormones flood his body, breathing becomes rapid and shallow, his heart pounds, and his muscles tense, ready for action. Riding the school bus, sitting at a desk in a classroom, taking a test, or spending hours in front of the TV or computer is not the kind of action his body has prepared for. It wants him to run away fast or go into battle. Only when physical activity is no longer necessary, or the brain gets the message that the danger has passed, do stress hormones decrease, allowing the body to return to its normal resting state.

If your child is stressed at school, then comes home and sits around for the rest of the day maybe worrying about homework he has to face or an upcoming test, he won't decrease stress hormones to low levels. They have no way to be released, so he will remain anxious. With the storm of the fight or flight raging, even at low levels, the ability to concentrate on homework and studying is difficult. But turning off the TV and turning on to exercise can make for a positive change.

How Does Exercise Benefit My Child?

Physical activity and exercise are not the same. Physical activity, like playing a game of tag, is not structured in the same way exercise is, and most children are active by playing and doing things like bike riding. Others are involved in formal programs, for example, martial arts, gymnastics, sports, and yoga classes. Nevertheless, whether your child engages in physical play or an exercise program, the benefits of physical movement will help your child cope with stress and reduce anxiety.

The positive benefits of exercise include getting fit and losing weight or maintaining proper weight, with long-term benefits of preventing and fighting conditions and diseases such as high blood pressure and heart disease. Regular exercise improves brain function, too, such as improvement of mood, feeling confident, and an increased ability to focus and concentrate, all important characteristics for success in school.

Positive Changes in the Brain

Physical activity affects mental functions including emotions, thought, memory, and learning through a complex combination of factors, some of which are discussed next. Research on this mind-body link is ongoing.

In the 1970s, federal government researchers and other major health organizations found that sustained physical exercise increases certain chemicals in the body called endogenous opioids, which have morphinelike qualities. One of these chemicals, called endorphins, is associated with the brain's hypothalamus and limbic systems, which aid in controlling emotions and behavior. Increases in these chemicals improve mood and act as natural painkillers.

Another area of research targets imbalances in the brain's neurotransmitters—dopamine, serotonin, and norepinephrine—which are associated with anxiety disorders and depression. Vigorous exercise seems to do what some antidepressants do—increase the levels of these chemicals while decreasing mental stress and positively enhancing mood. Stress hormones such as cortisol, which are involved in the fight-or-flight response, are also decreased through exercise.

Ongoing studies by the federal government and major research centers on the effects of exercise and cognitive function in children have found that thirty minutes of jogging two to three times a week significantly improves scores on cognitive function tests, but scores are lowered when the exercise stops. Cognitive functions include learning new concepts, using memory in studying, being able to handle homework and testing, and learning socialization skills.

The brain is a hungry organ, using up to 30 percent of a body's daily caloric intake and requiring quite a lot of oxygen to function well. Aerobic exercise, like walking, running, and bike riding, increases oxygen levels in the brain, which in turn increase body temperature, resulting in a lift in mood, a decrease in anxiety states, and feelings of well-being.

Boosting Self-Confidence

How children think about and see themselves in relation to the world has a major influence on their self-esteem and self-confidence, which impacts their emotions, habits, behaviors, and even life choices. Many students with school anxiety feel isolated from peers due to the struggle with their emotions. Because most of these students have to contend with low self-worth too, they often describe themselves as "dumb," "different," "ugly," "strange," or "weak." If their anxiety is obvious, other students may tease them about being "stupid," "weird," and call them names like "loser." Many children with chronic school anxiety cycle into depression and withdraw from interacting with peers, exacerbating the problem.

Low self-esteem and poor body image go hand in hand for anxious children. Becoming physically fit, or learning how to do a type of activity like tai chi or a sport like soccer can lead to increased self-confidence. For an anxious child who is isolated from peers and feels bad about himself, these changes will positively affect his school experience.

Children who are underweight or overweight, or who have obvious physical disabilities, are often teased mercilessly by classmates about their appearance, making being at school the last place on earth they want to be. These children may feel much safer at home and not wish to participate in physical activities or play with other children. They come home and want to plop in front of the TV or computer—great distractions from the pain of going to school. If your child fits into this category you want to get him up and out, but it will take patience to do so. You can start by routinely taking a walk with him every day after school. Or have him help you around the house cleaning, or involve him in home improvement projects, giving him time spent with you and a sense of accomplishment.

Increasing Social Interactions

School anxiety creates feelings of being different from family members and peers. Anxiety is an isolating condition and children who suffer often feel shame that they have these feelings or are unable to be like the other kids in the class. So, it is not uncommon for anxious children to feel alone and withdraw from social interaction as they struggle to cope with their inner fears. Becoming physically active is one way to create opportunities for your child to interact with other children, whether it is playing tag with neighborhood friends or joining in games at recess or being part of a team sport.

Engaging with the World Outside

Coping with anxiety and its symptoms can be a painful internal process. Anxious children dwell on their fears and symptoms such as stomachaches, headaches, racing heartbeat, and the feelings of dread and panic. Many children expend energy trying to avoid fearful situations such as going to school and test taking. Engaging in physical activity not only provides a distraction for anxious thinking but allows your child to change his focus to the external environment—the fun of playing with others and doing something creative and pleasurable. Don't force your child to participate if he resists, but slowly guide him to become engaged and active.

What Are the Types of Physical Activity and Exercise?

There are three types of physical activity: aerobic, anaerobic, and stretching. All three are important in a holistic health program and have a part to play in helping your child manage stress, reduce anxiety, maintain proper weight, become physically fit, and have overall good mental and physical health.

Aerobic Activity

Aerobic exercise is what children do when they engage in play such as running and swimming. If your child helps you garden or rake leaves, dances around the living room, or goes for a brisk walk with you after dinner, that too is aerobic activity. Aerobic means "with oxygen," and it describes a sustained exercise where heart rate and breathing are increased so muscles can use oxygen to change glucose, a simple sugar obtained in food and needed for energy, and fat into energy. Other aerobic activities that are good for your child include:

- Jogging
- Soccer
- Jumping, jumping rope, and hopscotch
- Gymnastics and tumbling

- Playing tag
- Kickball
- Bike riding

Aerobic activity will help your child maintain a good weight, increase his physical and mental stamina, improve his ability to manage stress at home and at school, pump up and strengthen the heart, lower blood sugar levels, and reduce the risk of type 2 diabetes. Finally, it just feels good to run around and get the blood pumping.

Anaerobic Activity

Anaerobic means "without oxygen," and this activity involves short periods of strenuous muscular activity followed by rest periods. This type of activity builds, strengthens, and tones muscles with exercises that include weight lifting and sit-ups. Some experts do not recommend formal strength training for children, whereas others disagree as long as it is closely monitored by educated adults. Anaerobic activities for children include climbing playground equipment, carrying heavy items like shopping bags, and helping with gardening and housecleaning. Anaerobic sports include baseball, downhill skiing, and wrestling. Having your child help you to clean windows or wash your family vehicle are forms of anaerobic activities, too.

Stretching

Anyone at any age can stretch. Stretching increases the length of muscles and tendons, which are cords of fibrous tissue that connects muscles to bones. Stretching is beneficial to both mind and body in the following ways:

- Reduces muscle tension, which decreases the mental grip of anxiety
- Increases muscular coordination
- Increases blood circulation to parts of the body
- Increases range of motion in joints
- Feels good

Stretching also helps prevent injuries during vigorous physical activity and increases energy levels due to enhanced blood circulation. Stretching is a natural phenomenon, so when your child wakes up in the morning the first thing she might do is stretch her arms over her head to get her body going. Your child likely stretches at her desk at school after she's been sitting for a while by wiggling around in her seat. School-anxious children can be taught simple stretching exercises as a self-calming technique to use during fearful situations, such as leaving home or being afraid to answer questions in class. Books with stretching exercises for children are listed in the resources section at the end of the book.

Structured Sports and Exercise Programs

You may want to have your child participate in an exercise or sports program for physical fitness, but many of these activities also provide other benefits, such as building confidence and learning how to play with others. Your child's developmental stage and level of maturity will determine the activities she can participate in. Some of the following activities can be started for children under a year old, and "Mommy and Me" and family classes are available for activities such as swimming, tumbling, and yoga.

- *Tumbling and Gymnastics*—kids learn forward and backward rolls, cartwheels, and so on.
- *Martial Arts*—include various types of karate and judo.
- *Dancing*—includes ballet, tap, jazz, and hip-hop.
- *Swimming*—the American Academy of Pediatricians advises that most children are developmentally ready for formal swim lessons by age five.
- *Sports*—includes T-ball, baseball, soccer, basketball, field hockey, football, tennis, skiing, and wrestling.
- *Yoga*—besides physical and other benefits, teaches mind-body connection and relaxation.

Participating in any of these activities can help your child develop a healthy and strong body and a lifelong commitment to being physically active. The abilities to be disciplined and to concentrate and focus are part of learning a sport or physical activity. Physical coordination, stamina, and balance are developed while practicing many of these activities. Dance offers children a way to express themselves and yoga helps children understand how their bodies work, and how to manage stressful situations.

> When Bill was in fourth grade, he was shy and overweight. He had few friends in school and was regularly teased about his weight by a group of boys in his class and some of the girls, too. He responded to the teasing by blushing and turning away from the group. However, during the summer before fifth grade, Bill joined a karate school. By the time he began fifth grade, he had lost some weight, which he felt good about, but more important, karate taught him to carry himself with confidence, which showed on the first day of fifth grade. When the bullies approached him, instead of blushing and turning away, Bill confronted them head-on. Not only did they stop teasing him, but a few of the boys asked him if he wanted to play with them at recess.

When shopping for a program or sport, keep in mind the following suggestions: Look for a positive philosophy from teachers and coaches; make sure teachers and coaches have the skills to work with children; find programs that are fun and reinforce "effort" as winning instead of promoting a cutthroat competitive philosophy; ask for a free trial run before you sign on.

✎ Guidelines for Getting Physical with Your Child

Involving your child in regular physical activity, either informally or formally, depends on circumstances and his desire to do so. Do not push him into an activity; you want to engage his interest, and for him to enjoy it. The guidelines listed next give you suggestions. Always contact your family physician before starting an exercise program.

1. Consult the U.S. Government's Council for Physical Education for Children to determine the minimum amount of daily activity recommended for your child.

2. Assess your child's activity level and your family's, too.

3. Be determined to make physical activity part of regular family life. Be a role model for your child. Have all family members cut down on passive exercise like watching TV or playing on the computer. Instead, get your family moving. For example, put on music and have everyone get up and dance.

4. Children have short attention spans, so plan for that in structured activities.

5. Use household chores or family projects as enjoyable physically active time with family members working together and feeling proud about a job well done.

6. Allow your child to have unstructured playtime, and don't overload his schedule or the family's with formal extracurricular activities.

Other suggestions include planning activities like nature walks, hiking, camping, biking, swimming, or skiing that the whole family enjoys and pursue them on a regular basis. Get a family membership at the local YMCA or health club. Above all, teach your child that physical activity is fun. Along with changing your level of physical activity, make dietary changes too. Have your child help you with this, assisting in looking for healthy recipes, shopping for the food, and cooking it. Refer to Chapter 17, "Eat Right to Feel Right," for information on nutrition.

ᏊᎧ

Making regular physical activity a part of your child's school anxiety program has no downside, only benefits. Being active feels good and releases stress. Participating in a class such as karate or dance teaches discipline and leads to feelings of having accomplished something. Getting fit helps with weight control and builds muscle and strength. These accomplishments in turn lead to increased confidence. A strong, confident child has a greater chance of being able to successfully cultivate good peer relationships; to handle daily stress; and to meet the school challenges of learning, homework, studying, and testing.

CHAPTER 19

What Are Traditional Medical Treatments for Children?

୧୬

DECIDING ON WHAT KIND OF TREATMENT IS BEST FOR YOUR anxious child can be a daunting task. Questions about the benefits of psychotherapy and the safety and use of medications for children are important and require answers. Your health-care providers may have differing opinions, making it tough for you to decide on a type of treatment. In this chapter, you will find an overview of the current traditional medical treatments for children.

What Are the Traditional Treatments?

The traditional mental health treatments for children are some form of therapy, psychotropic medications, or a combination of both. Educating yourself about the available treatments will allow you to ask the necessary questions when you meet with your family physician and mental heath professional.

What Are the Therapies That Treat Children?

Many therapies today are beneficial in treating children. The major variables that determine which methods will benefit your child are age and presenting problem. For example, Dale, a five-year-old kindergartner with separation anxiety disorder, works with a therapist who specializes in play therapy because as a young child he communicates much easier through play, his main mode of communication. On the other hand, Mandy, an eleven-year-old fifth grader, has the ability to fully engage in talk therapy, but age-appropriate play, board games, and art therapy are important components in her therapy too. Some therapists specialize in treating certain mental disorders, such as attention-deficit/hyperactivity disorder, and anxiety disorders.

What Is Play Therapy?

Therapists who specialize in play therapy use "play" as a way of speaking a child's language. Child's play is important, for it is how children learn about the world and communicate with it, express their thoughts, feelings, and emotions. Play teaches children how to develop physical, mental, and social skills. Play therapists create a safe environment to allow a child to build trust and open up emotionally. Therapists may engage in play with the child, watch the child play alone, or observe how the child plays with family members. Then the therapist interprets through the child's interactions, drawings, and stories what the child is feeling, attempting to learn, or trying to express. Play therapy can be nondirective, where the therapist lets the child take the lead, or the therapist may take a more direct, active approach. Play therapy is also used as a diagnostic tool during the initial evaluation.

The play therapy room is furnished with a variety of toys, games, and materials chosen specifically by the therapist, such as dolls and figures, dollhouses and furnishings, buildings, trees, toy kitchen appliances, dishes, pots, pans, toy cars, trucks, boats, soldiers, toy guns, knives and military equipment, plastic animals, stuffed animals, building materials, Erector Sets, art supplies, clay/Play-Doh, blackboard, chalk, musical instruments, board games, and cards.

Therapists also read with children, do poetry, puppetry, and play "dress up" in costumes, allowing children to creatively express themselves and reveal their problems. The play therapy room becomes for the child a microcosm of his larger world. In this room with this caring adult, a child can safely act out his anxieties, worries, and fears, something he may not be able to do outside of the therapy room.

What Are the Types of Play Therapy?

Children's play therapists differ in their interpretations of the child's play based on their theoretical models, and there are dozens of psychotherapeutic approaches to therapy. How the therapist interacts with the child, and which toys, games, and materials are offered in the therapy room vary, too.

What Are the Most Common Theoretical Models for Play Therapy?

The theories that are explained in this section are not necessarily play therapy theories but have been adapted for that use. Many therapists today call themselves "eclectic," meaning that though they were trained in a specific theoretical model, they use more than one mode of therapy in treatment, depending on the needs of the client. For example, a psychoanalytical therapist may also use behavioral techniques.

Some therapies are psychodynamically oriented, meaning that the therapist attempts to understand the conscious and unconscious issues that underlie a child's thoughts, feelings, and behavior, and helps the child to come to terms with unresolved issues. Focus is also placed on teaching the child coping skills to change negative patterns of behavior. The behavioral therapies emphasize the patient's present behavior that is causing distress, and then comes up with strategies to change that.

Cognitive-Behavioral Therapy

Cognitive-behavioral therapy (CBT) focuses on helping a child become aware of distorted thought patterns, attitudes, and beliefs that negatively influence reactions and behaviors. The therapist then teaches the child how to replace those negative thoughts and behaviors with more positive thoughts and appropriate ways to respond. Play therapists who use CBT take an active and directive role during sessions.

Rational-Emotive Therapy

Rational-emotive therapy (RET) looks at how irrational thinking creates self-defeating behaviors and life problems. The RET therapist is very active in therapy sessions, helping children to solve their behavior problems through play, and teaching them to look at circumstances and events rationally.

Child-Centered Play Therapy

In child-centered play therapy (CCPT), the therapist creates a nonjudgmental, supportive environment; builds a positive rapport and therapeutic relationship with the child; and establishes defined boundaries in which the child can learn how to control thoughts, feelings, and behaviors. CCPT therapists are nondirective, letting the child take the lead in choice of play materials.

Jungian Play Therapy

Jungian play therapy focuses on healing the psyche through the relationship of the child and therapist. Nondirective and semidirective methods using play, drawings, and sand tray tableaus. Then the therapist interprets the results symbolically to determine what the child has unconsciously repressed and helps the child work through the repressed issues.

Other Therapies

Other theories include filial therapy, where parents are present in the sessions and learn basic therapeutic play skills. Object relations and attachment therapies focus on the emotional bond, or lack thereof, between parent and child. Family therapy views the entire family as an entity for treatment, not just the child, and focuses on helping families build strong relationships and learn positive patterns of communication. Group therapy enables children to work out feelings in a safe environment and learn coping skills by interacting with their peers who face similar difficulties.

No matter which therapeutic model a therapist practices under, it is the personality of the therapist that is crucial for a positive outcome in treatment. The therapist has to be kind, nonjudgmental, and attentive; be able to develop a trusting relationship with the child; and be open to parents' questions, comments, and concerns.

Who Are the Therapists?

If you are thinking of finding a therapist for your child, it is important to be familiar with the types of therapists you will come in contact with and what their degrees mean. Determining if a therapist is right for your child does not depend on a specific degree. That will have to be determined with either a phone interview or most likely an initial meeting.

A therapist with a master's degree graduated from a two-year program. A doctorate takes at least four years of schooling. Psychologist degrees include Doctor of Philosophy (Ph.D.), Doctor of Psychology (Psy.D.), Doctor of Education (Ed.D.), Master's of Science (MS), and Master's of Art (MA). Social workers have studied either clinical social work or social policy, and their degrees include Doctor of Social Work (DSW) or Master's of Social Work (MSW). Marriage and family therapists and professional counselors may have any of the degrees listed here. Psychiatrists are medical doctors (MDs) with a specialty in psychiatry; child psychiatry is a subspecialty. Psychiatrists are experts in diagnosing mental conditions and the dispensing of psychotropic drugs; many practice psychotherapy too. All psychiatrists must be state licensed and most states require mental health clinicians to be licensed now, too. Licensing means the practitioner practices from a code of ethics, has to complete continuing education courses for license renewal, and is accountable to a state board.

What Are Psychotropic Medications?

Psychotropic medications are chemicals used to treat mental illness and emotional disorders by changing moods, feelings, and thoughts with the intention of altering behavior. In the last decade, there has been a steady increase in prescribing medication for young children with emotional and behavioral problems, such as attention-deficit disorders, anxiety disorders, obsessive-compulsive behavior, sleep problems, and depression.

Sometimes a physician will do something called "off label" prescribing, which the Food and Drug Administration (FDA) defines as "the use of a prescription drug for an indication, dosage form, dose regimen, population, or other use not mentioned in the approved labeling." If your child is prescribed a psychotropic medication, it is crucial you understand what the drug is intended to do, its side effects, recommendations regarding usage in children, and other pertinent safety information. A lack of adequate research on the possible negative effects of these drugs on a child's developing brain is a continuing concern in the mental health community. Here is an overview of psychotropic medications.

Antidepressants

Selective serotonin reuptake inhibitors (SSRIs) help the brain to maintain normal levels of the neurotransmitter serotonin, which affects mood. These drugs are used to treat depression, panic disorder, social phobia, and obsessive-compulsive disorder. Commonly known SSRIs are Prozac, Zoloft, Paxil, Effexor, Celexa, and Lexapro. Side effects include headaches, stomachache and nausea, sleep difficulty, anxiety, and agitation.

Other antidepressants include the older versions that are not as commonly prescribed as SSRIs and affect a number of brain chemicals. They are the atypical antidepressants Wellbutrin, Serzone, and the tricyclic antidepressants (TCAs) such as Elavil, Anafranil, and Tofranil. Monoamine oxidase inhibitors (MAOIs) include Nardil and Pamate. Side effects may include increased anxiety, night sweats, restlessness, insomnia, blurry vision, and loss of concentration, and there may be dietary restrictions.

In 2004, the FDA issued a warning that now appears on all SSRI labels that antidepressants may increase the risk of suicidal ideation (thinking about it) and suicidal behavior (trying it) in some children.

Stimulants and Nonstimulants

Stimulants are medications used to treat attention-deficit/hyperactivity disorder (ADHD). It is unclear how these drugs, called psychostimulants, work, but when effective, they increase a child's ability to focus and ignore distractions. Common names are Adderall and Adderall XR, Concerta, Dexadrine, Focalin, Metadate CD and Metadate ER, Methylin, and Ritalin and Ritalin LA. An FDA-approved nonstimulant for treating ADHD is Strattera. Side effects include decreased appetite, weight loss, headaches, stomachaches, feeling jittery, social withdrawal, and sleep problems.

Benzodiazepines—Antianxiety Medications

Antianxiety medications are part of the tranquilizer and sleeping pill family that work by suppressing the central nervous system, which lessens feelings of anxiety. These drugs are fast acting, prescribed for severe anxiety, and intended for short-term use because they can be highly addictive. Common antianxiety drugs are Xanax, Ativan, Valium, and Klonopin. Other antianxiety drugs include antihistamines such as Benadryl and Vistaril. Atypical antianxiety drugs are BuSpar and Ambien. Side effects include dependency with long-term use. The withdrawal symptoms can create problems such as severe anxiety, depression, irritability, heart palpitations, shaking, and panic attacks, so dosage is reduced gradually when discontinuing use in order to lessen these symptoms.

Other Medications Used to Treat Children

Sleep problems are treated with Desyrel, Ambien, and Benadryl. Antipsychotic medications such as Haldol, Thorazine, Risperdal, and Clozaril have been used to treat severe anxiety and aggressive behavior. Severe mood swings and bipolar disorder are treated with mood stabilizers and anticonvulsants that include Lithium, Depakote, and Tegretol.

৩৩

Treating children with psychotropic medication is common practice today. If it is recommended that your child start on a course of drugs, it is incumbent on you to do your homework before your child begins treatment, have questions ready for your physician, and make sure that you receive information on the drug's studies for side effects and long-term consequences for children.

What Steps Do I Take to Get My Child into Treatment?

To determine the best type of treatment or combination of treatment options, it is important to get as accurate a diagnosis as you can. Sometimes that can be difficult given the complex nature of mental and behavioral problems. Many childhood problems can be treated successfully with therapy alone, such as anxiety disorders and social problems. If a course of medication is indicated, most physicians will recommend the child see a therapist too. To navigate the steps toward getting help for your child follow these guidelines:

1. Make an appointment with your family physician to have your child get a complete physical exam, which may include blood tests to determine if a medical condition is causing symptoms.
2. Before you see your family physician write down pertinent information about your child's condition, for example, when it began, symptoms and behaviors, and specify what is happening.
3. Attempt to elicit information about what is bothering your child in a gentle, caring, nonjudgmental manner.
4. Talk to your child about seeking treatment. Tell her what to expect and who she is going to see to alleviate any fears she may have.
5. Keep the school informed of the steps you are taking, and get feedback from school personnel about your child's academic and social behavior in class. Take that information to your child's doctor or therapist.

6. Include appropriate family members in your child's treatment for best results.

How Do I Find a Child Therapist?

If you decide that your child needs therapy, it is important that you find the right therapist for your child. The following guidelines can help:

1. Get referrals from your family physician, pediatrician, and school personnel. Ask other parents whose children have been in treatment for recommendations.
2. Call as many therapists as possible and ask them about their education and experience in treating children with similar problems. Look for licensed therapists with at least a master's degree.
3. Ask about insurance coverage and fees.
4. Question therapists on their therapeutic approach, and ask them how they would work with your child on his particular problem.
5. Ask the therapist to describe what generally happens in therapy sessions. Ask how parents are included and supported during your child's treatment. Find out how the therapist will handle problems in therapy sessions, such as your child not wanting to go into the therapy room without you or not wanting to engage with the therapist.
6. During the phone interview and at the first session, be aware how you feel about the therapist's approach to you: Is the therapist engaging, forthcoming, and open about his or her work? How will the therapist keep you informed and part of the process? If you are not satisfied, find another therapist.

The first job of the therapist is to ease your child's anxiety about being in treatment, and to work on building a trusting relationship so that your child is free to express herself and begin the process of therapeutic healing.

What Happens in Child Therapy?

After you decide on a therapist, you may be asked to come in alone for the first session so the therapist can discuss the specifics of your child's problem and to get a detailed family history. Some therapists want to see the child during the first session. This will depend on your child's problem, age, and so forth. At the therapist's office, you will show your insurance card and most likely have to fill out forms, which could include a release-of-information form, so your therapist can contact the school and family physician for information from them about your child.

The best therapy is one based on consistency, so sessions will normally take place once a week, and at the same time. The therapist's first task is to get to know your child, and he or she will also introduce your child to the playroom and explain the rules, for example, that the child can choose what to play with, that toys have to be put away at the end of the session, that her drawings and paintings will go into her own special folder, and so on.

The same guidelines as for seeking a therapist can be used if you are seeking psychiatric care for your child. And it is important to remember that you have the right to question any health-care provider about your child's treatment, get updates on your child's progress, and discuss with the provider any concerns you have about how the provider interacts with your child or yourself. You are the parent and the consumer, so do not hesitate to exercise your rights.

CHAPTER 20

What Are Alternative Treatments for Children?

෬෨

C OMPLEMENTARY AND ALTERNATIVE MEDICINE (CAM), such as the use of vitamins, meditation, acupuncture, and body work, has slowly become accepted for the treatment of physical ailments and emotional distress by a majority of the medical community. In fact, over the centuries these alternative therapeutics were the medicines of their day, such as the use of herbs to treat disease and mental stress. CAM is also being used to treat children for various physical and emotional conditions. According to Dr. Andrew Weil, "complementary medicine" combines the best of alternative and traditional medicine.

Benny, a third grader who was diagnosed with ADHD, has trouble concentrating in class and on tests, so he has become anxious. He is now enrolled in yoga class and is learning to calm himself and focus on his schoolwork.

Kara, in fifth grade, has generalized anxiety disorder and is on antidepressant medication, but she also goes to an acupuncturist and massage therapist to ease her anxiety in hopes of going off the medication someday.

This chapter defines complementary and alternative medicine and gives an overview of the specific treatments used for children, and the practitioners who utilize these treatments. The information in this chapter is not intended as an endorsement of CAM treatments. If you are interested in exploring this avenue of treatment do your homework and discuss it with your health-care provider first.

What Do Complementary and Alternative Mean?

The practice of complementary and alternative medicine is also called mind-body medicine. Its philosophy is that all body systems and functions are interdependent, and that problems in one area of the mind or body will affect overall health. Treatments are considered holistic. CAM body techniques and preparations act on the mind to boost the immune system so the body's own resources can heal physical disease and emotional disorders.

Complementary medicine refers to treatments that are used together with conventional medicine, for example, combining therapeutic massage with medication and psychotherapy to treat anxiety. Alternative remedies are used instead of traditional treatments, such as being treated by a homeopathic physician who prescribes specific compounds to heal stress and anxiety, as opposed to seeing a psychiatrist and taking tranquilizers.

The acceptance of CAM in conventional medical treatment has taken decades and is the result of people becoming aware of alternative treatments through popular culture, a desire for mind-body remedies, and the realization that conventional medicines do not always prove effective, and often have harsh side effects. The American Medical Association (AMA) and other organizations have done studies that show large percentages of Americans spend billions of dollars on alternative medical treatment.

Today, almost all of the major university medical centers, such as Johns Hopkins, UCLA, and the University of Pennsylvania, have CAM centers for research and treatment. It is not clear to medical experts how many CAM treatments work, and research on the efficacy and safety of complementary and alternative treatments for the conditions and diseases for which they are used is ongoing. Research on the benefits of CAM remedies for children's conditions is small, but growing too. Books on the use of CAM treatments for children are included in the resources section of the book.

What Is Integrative Medicine?

The term *integrative medicine* is used when the mode of treatment is the combination of conventional medical treatments and CAM therapies that have been researched and shown to have some scientific evidence of success and safety, such as therapeutic massage and diet. An integrative medical practitioner promotes the prevention of illness with lifestyle changes and works with the patient in a partnership that treats the patient holistically in mind, body, spirit, and community.

What Are CAM Methods?

Complementary and alternative practices, systems, and products are divided into five areas of practice: biologically based remedies, mind-body interventions, energy therapies, whole-medicine systems, and manipulative body-based practices. Since all CAM treatments are based on mind-body philosophy, they overlap from one area of practice to another. For example, chiropractic medicine is found under whole-medicine systems as well as manipulative body-based practices.

What Are Biologically Based Therapies?

Biologically based therapies are remedies that use materials found in nature and can be ingested, massaged into the skin, or delivered by other means, such as smell. Many of these therapies and ingredients are used to reduce stress and anxiety and are being given to children, such as large doses of vitamins. Remember, there is no scientific proof that CAM therapies work or that they are safe for children. Following are some of the commonly known remedies.

Dietary Supplements, Vitamins, and Nutrition

Dietary supplements are products that may contain a combination of vitamins, minerals, herbs, plant and animal products, enzymes, amino acids, and other ingredients that are used to "supplement" the diet and improve health. Supplements are regulated by the FDA using a set of guidelines that differ from those that cover food, prescriptions, and over-the-counter medications. No standards exist for purity and safe dosage, but the FDA states that the manufacturer is responsible for safety, truth-in-label information, and health claims.

The most common supplements given to children are vitamins, which are considered CAM therapies when megadoses are given outside of the conventional doses recommended by federal guidelines. Other popular supplements include garlic, fish oil, and probiotics, which are the so-called good bacteria found in or added to food such as yogurt, and herbs, like echinacea, which is believed to strengthen the immune system and ward off disease.

Herbs

Humans have depended on herbs as the primary source of medicine for thousands of years. Herbs are widely used in the United States in conjunction with conventional medicine, or as stand-alone treatments, for example, drinking chamomile tea to soothe a stomachache and calm nerves. The following herbs are commonly known for use in the treatment of anxiety-related conditions. Check with your physician or homeopathic doctor before administering these or any herbs to your child: Passionflower is used to decrease anxiety and hyperactivity, reduce insomnia, calm nerves, and lower blood pressure. Valerian has sedative-like qualities and is used to treat anxiety and insomnia. Lavender has sedative qualities and is used both internally and externally to treat anxiety, insomnia, and restlessness. It is considered a natural remedy for panic attacks.

Herbs have to be used with caution for reasons that include side effects and allergic conditions, dosage and frequency, and interactions with drugs and certain foods. If your child is taking prescription or over-the-counter medications, check with a physician before administering herbs. Thoroughly research any herb you are considering using.

Bach Flower Therapy

Bach Flower Therapy is considered a type of "energy medicine," in which flower essences are mixed with water and then used to treat anxiety, phobias, depression, and other mental conditions. One popular remedy, Bach Flower Essences & Rescue Remedy, made up of clematis, impatiens, rockrose, star-of-Bethlehem, and cherry plum, is used to treat children's anxiety and behavior problems.

Aromatherapy

Aromatherapy uses the oils of certain plants whose scents are pleasing to positively affect mood by stimulating the nervous system. Oils may be inhaled, sprayed to scent an area, or added to a bath. Common plants used in aromatherapy are lavender, rose, peppermint, chamomile, and lemon balm. Aromatherapy is used to ease stress and tension, to reduce anxiety and relieve pain, and to increase mental energy.

What Is Mind-Body Medicine?

Mind-body medicine is based on mental techniques that are thought to positively act on the nervous system to impact bodily functions such as the immune system, endocrine gland system, and autonomic nervous system to promote healing, prevent physical and mental illness, and for general well-being. Mind-body techniques have been practiced for thousands of years and include relaxation techniques, meditation, yoga, hypnosis, and guided imagery. Some CAM treatments have become conventional treatments, such as cognitive-behavioral therapy, support groups, and biofeedback.

Breath Work

Breath work is the use of breathing patterns to bring about deep relaxation, which relieves tension and anxiety, helps promote clear thinking, and is beneficial for good physical and emotional health. Certain types of breathing, like diaphragmatic breathing, will keep stress hormones at low levels and increase the function of the immune system. Breath work can build confidence because it is a conscious method of taking control of anxiety and positively coping with life events.

Yoga

Through breathing techniques and postures, the practice of yoga is beneficial for taking control of anxiety, increasing the skills necessary to manage stress, and becoming physically fit. Today, yoga is main-streamed into our culture with yoga schools throughout the country. Yoga classes for children are growing in popularity. Yoga programs are also beginning to crop up in schools across the country to help children deal with stress, anxiety, and behavior problems. For more information on yoga for children, see Chapter 18, "Getting Physical with Your Child."

Relaxation Techniques

Relaxation techniques are important tools that can be used to handle daily stress and ease the symptoms of anxiety. There are many types of relaxation techniques, including slow diaphragmatic breathing, which engages the nervous system's relaxation response and stops the fight-or-flight response from occurring; progressive relaxation, which systematically relaxes muscles and alleviates body tension and eases mental stress; and hypnosis or self-hypnosis, the technique of using relaxation techniques to enter into an "altered mental state" where the therapist or you can make suggestions for positive change. All of these techniques are used with children who have anxiety, behavior problems, and physical illness. Some of the techniques are used in schools by guidance counselors and teachers.

Meditation

Meditation, also called mindfulness meditation, is a special form of relaxation that leads to increased awareness of mind and body, and the ability to stay in the moment—a potent technique for turning off anxious states. Meditation, like its counterpart yoga, is in the mainstream, and schools are offering it to help students deal with school stress.

What Is Energy Medicine?

Energy therapy specialists believe that physical and mental illnesses are caused by disturbances in a person's energy, and that correcting these imbalances will restore health. Veritable energy therapies include magnetic therapy, and millimeter wave therapy. Many of the energy therapies are being studied by major hospitals and research centers, but definitive scientific evidence of their benefits has not been proved.

Acupuncture, one of the most mainstreamed energy therapies, has been extensively studied and research shows it is effective in treating conditions such as chronic pain, but how it works remains elusive.

What Are Whole-Alternative-Medicine Systems?

Whole-medicine systems are more than a group of techniques; they are a structured approach to healing based on theory and practice that have developed outside of conventional medicine. These systems take a holistic mind-body view of the person. Many of these systems have been practiced outside of the Western world for thousands of years, such as Chinese medicine and Ayurvedic medicine from India, but others, such as homeopathy, evolved in the West.

Chinese Medicine

Traditional Chinese medicine (TCM), dating back to 200 B.C., is based on balancing two innate opposing forces found in humans—yin and yang. When these forces are out of balance, the flow of vital energy, or chi, is blocked and disease occurs. Practitioners of TCM use a variety of healing techniques including acupuncture; massage and body manipulation; and natural products such as herbs, as well as diet and exercise.

Ayurvedic Medicine

Ayurvedic medicine, meaning "the science of life," was developed in India centuries ago. Its therapeutic procedures are used to balance and heal a person physically, mentally, socially, and spiritually through breath work, diet, herbs, exercise, meditation, and being in sunlight. Ayurvedic medicine has developed treatments for physical diseases such as diabetes and heart conditions as well as stress-related mental conditions.

Naturopathy

Naturopathy, a system of healing, was developed in Europe in the early 1900s. Its basic premise is that disease occurs when the body's natural processes to heal itself are blocked. The core philosophy is to treat the whole person, to prevent disease, and to utilize the healing power of nature through diet, herbs, and nutritional supplements; Chinese medicine; massage; and counseling to help people make healthful lifestyle changes.

Homeopathy

Homeopathy emphasizes that health is a manifestation of a person's physical, emotional, and spiritual state. Homeopathy is considered a complementary medicine that treats physical and emotional illness with remedies made from plants, minerals, and insects. These preparations, taken in the form of pills, powders, ointments and liquids, are believed to stimulate the body's immune system and healing powers.

Chiropractic Medicine

Chiropractic medicine is complementary and alternative with a mind-body philosophy about disease. Chiropractors believe that misalignments of the spinal column interfere with the nervous system and cause physical and emotional poor health. By adjusting the spine and normalizing its relationship to the body, the power of the body to heal itself is released. By law, chiropractors cannot prescribe medication.

Osteopathy

Osteopathy, an alternative medicine like chiropractic medicine, is based on the premise that physical and mental dysfunction arises when the musculoskeletal system is out of balance with the rest of the body's functions and systems. Osteopaths may use hands-on techniques on the body to restore health, but are licensed to practice conventional medicine and can prescribe medication.

What Are Manipulative Body-Based Practices?

Manipulative body-based practices use movement or massage of parts of the body or its functions, such as the lymphatic and circulatory systems, soft tissues, and bones and joints, to help the body heal itself.

These practices include chiropractic and osteopathic medicine, massage, and a host of other techniques that include:

- *Reflexology*—usually foot massage, where pressure points are massaged to release the flow of energy to the body to decrease stress and increase well-being.
- *Alexander Technique*—a hands-on technique to improve posture through movement that teaches people how to use muscles effectively to promote physical health and psychological well-being.
- *Rolfing*—a type of deep massage of the connective tissue believed to balance the organs, bones, and joints, which will ease stress and increase physical and mental energy.
- *Trager Bodywork/Tragerwork*—a technique where practitioners use their hands to help clients release tension through the experience of moving freely through gentle rocking, stretching, shaking, and vibrating.
- *Shiatsu*—a form of massage using finger pressure that focuses on releasing the vital energy, or "chi," to the body's meridians, which will unblock chi, and allow mind and body to function in harmony.

Some of the many other types of massage and manipulative therapies, too many to list, include the Bowen Technique, a form of gentle massage of muscles and tendons; the Feldenkrais Method, which utilizes hands-on techniques and movement; and Tui Na, an acupoint massage using fingers and thumb on the body's energy meridians. Remember to research any of these techniques carefully and discuss them with your physician before having your child treated.

Who Are the CAM Practitioners?

CAM practitioners may have medical degrees, such as Doctor of Osteopathy or Doctor of Chiropractic medicine, and must be state licensed to practice. Others like acupuncturists and massage therapists may or may not be licensed depending on state law. In choosing a CAM practitioner, be selective in the same way you would in choosing your family physician. Interview the practitioners, asking them about their training and experience, license, fees, and insurance coverage. Get a referral from a reliable source such as your physician, hospital, health and wellness center, or mental health clinician.

The anxiety, mental stress, insecurity, and worries about going to and succeeding in school negatively affect your child's physical, mental, and emotional well-being. Your treatment plan should take into account a mind-body approach to heal your child from the grip of anxiety.

Wrap-Up

CONGRATULATIONS! YOU AND YOUR CHILD HAVE STARTED using the Overcoming School Anxiety Program, which could help him or her to become a self-assured student with a zest for learning. Maybe you and your child have read through the entire book and worked the program chapter by chapter. Or maybe you've decided to concentrate on specific problems and exercises. No matter which approach you chose, it is the discipline of daily practice, the patience you have with your child, and your belief in your child's ability to be able to overcome anxiety that will spell eventual success.

The basic steps to begin helping your child overcome school anxiety are recognizing that there is a problem if your child exhibits anxiety symptoms and behaviors; contacting the school to work together as a team; taking your child to your family physician and seeking help from a mental health specialist if anxiety persists; learning about anxiety and how to manage your own stress; de-stressing your household; and teaching your child how to face anxiety and to become proactive in taking control of it.

Children who spend their days trying to cope with anxiety generally feel frightened, isolated, helpless, shameful, small, and worthless. Anxiety can sap the energy and joy from their lives. The following quote attributed to Nelson Mandela made in his 1994 inaugural speech distills my philosophy about anxious children and drives my desire to help them:

Our deepest fear is not that we are inadequate. Our deepest fear is that we are powerful beyond measure. It is our light, not our darkness, that most frightens us. We ask ourselves, "Who am I to be brilliant, gorgeous, talented, and fabulous?" Actually, who are you not to be? You are a child of God. Your playing small doesn't serve the world. There's nothing enlightened about shrinking so that other people won't feel insecure around you.

Resources

Bennett, Sara, and Nancy Kalish. *The Case Against Homework: How Homework Is Hurting Our Children and What We Can Do About It.* New York: Crown, 2006.

Bersma, Daniella, Marjoke Visscher, and Alex Kooistra. *Yoga Games for Children: Fun and Fitness with Postures, Movements and Breath.* Alameda, CA: Hunter House, 2003.

Chansky, Tamar E. *Freeing Your Child from Anxiety: Powerful, Practical Solutions to Overcome Your Child's Fears, Worries and Phobias.* New York: Broadway, 2001.

Chivers, Maria. *Dyslexia and Alternative Therapies.* London: Jessica Kingsley Publishers, 2006.

Coloroso, Barbara. *The Bully, the Bullied, and the Bystander: From Preschool to High School—How Parents and Teachers Can Help Break the Cycle of Violence.* New York: Collins, 2004.

Dunn Buron, Kari. *When My Worries Get Too Big! A Relaxation Book for Children Who Live with Anxiety.* Shawnee Mission, KS: Autism Asperger Publishing, 2006.

Eisen, Andrew R., Linda B. Engler, and Joshua Sparrow. *Helping Your Child Overcome Separation Anxiety or School Refusal: A Step-by-Step Guide for Parents.* Oakland, CA: New Harbinger Publications, 2006.

Evers, Connie L. *How to Teach Nutrition to Kids*, 3rd ed. Portland, OR: 24 Carrot Press, 2006.

Gardner, Howard. *Five Minds for the Future.* Boston: Harvard Business School Press, 2007.

Gardner, Howard. *Intelligence Reframed: Multiple Intelligences for the 21st Century.* New York: Basic Books, 2000.

Gladstar, Rosemary. *Rosemary Gladstar's Herbal Remedies for Children's Health.* Pownal, VT: Storey Publishing, 1999.

Greespon, Thomas S. *Freeing Our Families from Perfectionism*. Minneapolis: Free Spirit Publishing, 2001.

Huebner, Dawn, and Bonnie Matthews. *What to Do When You Worry Too Much: A Kid's Guide to Overcoming Anxiety*. Washington, DC: Magination Press, 2006.

Kaufman, Gershen, Lev Raphael, and Pamela Espeland. *Stick Up for Yourself: Every Kid's Guide to Personal Power & Positive Self-Esteem*. Minneapolis: Free Spirit Publishing, 1999.

Kralove, Etta, and John Buell. *The End of Homework: How Homework Disrupts Families, Overburdens Children, and Limits Learning*. Boston: Beacon Press, 2001.

Leonhardt, Mary, and Molly Leonhardt. *99 Ways to Help Your Kids Love to Do Their Homework (and Not Hate It)*. New York: Three Rivers Press, 2000.

Luby, Thia. *Children's Book of Yoga: Games & Exercises Mimic Plants & Animals & Objects*. Santa Fe, NM: Clear Light Books, 1998.

Marianna Csoti, Maria. *School Phobia, Panic Attacks and Anxiety in Children*. London: Jessica Kingsley Publishers, 2003.

Pando, Nancy, and Kathy Voerg. *I Don't Want to Go to School: Helping Children Cope with Separation Anxiety (Let's Talk)*. Far Hills, NJ: New Horizon Press, 2005.

Plummer, Deborah M. *Helping Children to Build Self-Esteem: A Photocopiable Activities Book*, 2nd ed. London: Jessica Kingsley Publishers, 2007.

Romain, Trevor, and Elizabeth Verdeck. *How to Do Homework Without Throwing Up*. Minneapolis: Free Spirit Publishing, 1997.

Virgilio, Stephen J. *Active Start for Healthy Kids: Activities, Exercises, and Nutritional Tips*. Champaign, IL: Human Kinetics, 2006.

Websites

National Institute of Mental Health (NIMH), www.nimh.nih.gov

Anxiety Disorders Association of America, www.adaa.org

U.S. Department of Agriculture. Site designed for elementary school children with information and games about nutrition and physical activity, www.MyPyramid.gov

Index

About the Author

Diane Peters Mayer, a licensed social worker, has a bachelor's degree in psychology and a master's degree in clinical social work from the University of Pennsylvania. She has been a psychotherapist and performance anxiety coach in private practice in Doylestown, Pennsylvania, for eighteen years. A specialist in anxiety and anxiety disorders, Ms. Mayer works with adults, adolescents, and children. She developed her school anxiety program to address the stress and anxiety that are pervasive in both home and school today, and has helped hundreds of children to overcome anxiety, enabling them to achieve success in the learning environment.

Ms. Mayer is the author of *Conquering Ring Nerves* and *The Everything Health Guide to Controlling Anxiety*. She has two grown daughters and lives in Pennsylvania with her husband and a rescued beagle mix.